A Guide to How Your Child Learns

Brain Smart Series

The *Brain Smart* series consists of three books, offering readers a wide range of tools and information to support your child's learning brain. Using up-to-date research and hands-on learning strategies, parents can explore how their children learn at all grade levels.

A Guide to How Your Child Learns: Understanding the Brain from Infancy to Young Adulthood features sixty relevant and digestible articles on learning, while the second book explores the physiology of your child's brain, and the third provides the hands-on techniques needed to help improve development.

Together, these books explore important topics as memory consolidation, windows of opportunities, techniques to improve your student's attention span, multiple intelligence assessments, and give you the tools to define your child's specific cognitive stages, and help improve their study skills, test-taking ability, organization, listening, and critical thinking.

A Guide to How Your Child Learns

Understanding the Brain from Infancy to Young Adulthood

David P. Sortino, EdM, PhD

ROWMAN & LITTLEFIELD
Lanham • Boulder • New York • London

Published by Rowman & Littlefield
A wholly owned subsidary of The Rowman & Littlefield Publishing Group, Inc.
4501 Forbes Boulevard, Suite 200, Lanham, Maryland 20706
www.rowman.com

Unit A, Whitacre Mews, 26–34 Stannary Street, London SE11 4AB

British Library Cataloguing in Publication Information Available
A catalogue record for this book is available from the British Library
ISBN: HB 978-1-4758-3182-5

Library of Congress Cataloging-in-Publication Data

Names: Sortino, David P., author.
Title: A guide to how your child learns : understanding the brain from infancy to young
    adulthood / David P. Sortino.
Description: Lanham : Rowman & Littlefield, [2017] | Includes bibliographical refer-
    ences.
Identifiers: LCCN 2017040647 (print) | LCCN 2017047313 (ebook) | ISBN
    9781475831849 (Electronic) | ISBN 9781475831825 (cloth : alk. paper) | ISBN
    9781475831832 (pbk. : alk. paper)
Subjects: LCSH: Learning, Psychology of. | Learning—Physiological aspects. | Brain.
Classification: LCC LB1057 (ebook) | LCC LB1057 .S64 2017 (print) | DDC
    370.15/23—dc23
LC record available at https://lccn.loc.gov/2017040647

Printed in the United States of America

Contents

v

List of Articles

SECTION III: EARLY ADOLESCENCE: AGES ELEVEN TO SIXTEEN

> *Most of us remember adolescence as a kind of double negative: no longer*
> *allowed to be children, we are not yet capable of being adults.*

> —Julian Barnes

SECTION IV: LATE ADOLESCENCE TO EARLY ADULTHOOD: AGES SEVENTEEN TO EARLY TWENTIES

Acknowledgments

I want to thank editors Mr. Paul Gulixson and Mr. David Abbott from the Santa Rosa Press Democrat and the West County News for their encouragement and support during the writing of my book *A Guide to How Your Child Learns: Understanding the Brain from Infancy to Young Adulthood*. Without their support this book would never have come to completion.

In addition, special thanks to Mrs. Jan Corbett who provided incredible support and editing for the completion of this book.

Introduction

Our first section, Early Childhood: Ages Two to Six Years Old, chapter 1 addresses every teacher's and parent's nightmare: a kindergartener or first grader with weak or delayed printing or drawing (sensory-motor) skills. Delayed printing or drawing skills are often represented by inconsistent letter size of upper and lower case letters or with children's art, drawings consisting of circles that resemble squares or squares that resemble circles. Delayed printing or drawing may lead to delayed reading and language skills, possibly indicating the beginning stages of a struggling student.

In order to create what I like to call a better learning brain, students must be organized, adaptive, passionate, and secure about learning. Research and follow-up studies of these traits, with theoretical knowledge, may suggest why multiple intelligence, child development theory, learning styles, moral development and cognitive development should be included in every parent and or teacher's playbook.

For example, one very important challenge for teachers and parents with this age group is preserving and protecting elements of the magical child philosophy (fantasy and imagination), while, at the same time, expecting students to successfully transition to school learning, regardless of their ability or interest level. Walk into any school and observe the writing or artwork on the school's walls and you will see an incredible range of abilities and possible school success. These miraculous differences in abilities and learning styles need to be honored.

From early childhood, we proceed to Section II: Late Childhood: Ages Seven to Ten, with chapter 15, entitled, Developmental Delays and School Readiness. This article stresses why knowledge of cognitive development (how children think and learn) is a critical component for higher order thinking and learning.

A good example would be this fifth grade science lesson on species. The students are told to group the five animals based on similarities: cow, lion, hawk, bat, and dog. Ninety percent of the students group the animals according to walking and flying. These students are thinking at the concrete operational stage, the ability to entertain two ideas at one time. However, ten percent of the students see something different. This group is thinking at a formal operational stage or the ability to entertain three plus ideas at one time. They know that a bat is also a mammal, thus grouping their animals according to a higher operation of cognition.

The teacher's dilemma? How does one teach a formal operational lesson when ninety percent of the class is still thinking concretely? The teacher must think out of the box. A teacher could bring in a live bat attaching a different learning modality (intelligence) to the lesson. The potential result could be that all of her students will group according to species! The reasons for the students' improvement? When a teacher attaches another learning intelligence to a lesson (bringing in a live bat), she stimulates the student's limbic system or the hippocampus, seat of bonding, causing the higher centers of her student's learning brain to achieve greater learning.

Section III: Early Adolescence: Ages Eleven to Sixteen, includes chapter 32, Transitioning to Middle School. This chapter describes a common middle schooler's dilemma. It is as though the student has worked six or seven years at the same company and now must move to another company. Instead of one boss, he now has five or six bosses. Instead of working in one office for most of the day, he must move every hour to other offices five or six times a day! If he is late getting to any of his offices, the punishment could be time spent in his office after work with other tardy workers.

Middle school should serve as a bridge to high school. To cross this bridge, teachers and parents must minimize your student's stress with the transition. In other words, negative experiences have the potential to provoke a reaction from the student's emotional midbrain (amygdala) into a fight or flight response, short-circuiting possible higher order thinking, and social intelligence. To deal with this problem, middle school teachers and parents need to teach a crash course in basic adjustments to middle school life. For instance, they should teach students how to open lockers without being late for class or how to deal with more serious psycho-physiological problems, such as differences on maturity rates. That is, some boys will be five feet tall and look like fourth graders, while others are six feet tall and already shaving. Further, some girls will have yet to reach puberty, while others look more like a grown woman than a child.

Our final Section IV: Late Adolescence: Early Adulthood: Ages Seventeen to Early Twenties includes chapter 45, Vocational Intelligence – Just Ask Bill Gates. This timeless article addresses why this group often views the transition to adulthood with severe trepidation. Do I go to college or pursue a vocation? These students are actually the lucky ones! Another group does not have a clue as to their potential education and vocational opportunities.

Bottom line: all groups would benefit from a vocational assessment that could help stimulate an emotional bond with a vocation or interest. In other words, if we provide this age group with a vocational identity, we provide their brains with the opportunity to bond with this potential. Again, the development of a vocational identity moves this age group away from the fear of the unknown and a fight or flight response, thus allowing the executive brain centers to bond with a vocation.

Question? Why wait until late adolescence or early adulthood to create a student's vocational identity. Children display their vocational interests early in life through play and social interactions. Bill Gates began to develop a vocational identity as a high school student. At age six, Steven Spielberg asked for a camera so he could make family movies. It is never too early to begin to feed the child's vocational interests.

A Guide to How Your Child Learns: Understanding the Brain from Infancy to Young Adulthood represents my first of three books in the Brain Smart series. This first book asks parents and teachers to think out of the box and look at the learning brain differently. Moreover, when you read my concise chapters, you are actually stepping into the shoes of a learning specialist that spans almost forty years.

The model has already been created and demonstrated by many successful individuals. Hopefully, my book will provide readers with pathways for creating intelligent models for learners of all ages and abilities.

—David P. Sortino, EdM, PhD (2017)

Section I

EARLY CHILDHOOD

Figure 1.1 A Group of Preschoolers in a Line.
istock.com/PhotoEuphoria

AGES TWO TO SIX: PRESCHOOL TO KINDERGARTEN

It's a beautiful day in this neighborhood,
A beautiful day for a neighbor.
Would you be mine?
Could you be mine?

—Mr. Rogers

The early childhood stage represents roughly ages two to six years, with two sub-stages, ages two to four and four to six. The brain's cerebellum plays a dominant role in the behavior of this age group as it attaches the child's need for sensory/motor activities to his kinesthetic intelligence.

Further, the first sub-stage, about ages two to four, is also associated with what brain scientists like to call the first renaissance or when the brain's development begins to move (bottom to top) to the emotional midbrain or limbic system. In fact, the terrible twos are nothing more than the child's cerebellum and kinesthetic intelligence asking for more movement, while the immature emotional midbrain (limbic system) fights parental controls with tantrums and loud *nos*! Although the entire brain is in play, again it is an endless struggle between the sensory/motor or the child's kinesthetic needs to dominate, while the immature emotional midbrain becomes frustrated by parental controls that lead to tantrums and/or emotional meltdowns.

Therefore, find a good preschool program that integrates the arts with sensory/motor skills. Also reinforce this learning with a home environment that supports the arts and sensory/motor activities, and you will begin to establish a positive learning experience that can lead to higher order learning. The saying *I learned it by heart* is nothing more than creating a learning environment that links passion with learning.

Chapter 1

Delayed Printing Skills—What Should Parents Do?

What should parents do when they notice their kindergartener or first grader has weak or delayed printing or drawing (sensory-motor) skills? Delayed printing or drawing skills are often represented by inconsistent letter size of upper and lower case letters or with children's drawings—circles that resemble squares or squares that resemble circles. Now compare delayed printing or drawing to reading and language arts delays and you begin to see the potential for a struggling student.

For example, Edwards, L. (2003) in "Writing Instruction in Kindergarten: Examining an Emerging Area of Research for Children with Writing and Reading Difficulties" (*Journal of Learning Disabilities*, Vol. 36, No. 2, pp. 136–148). This review examines the literature on how to teach kindergarten children with reading and writing difficulties how to write, and reports that *text production* is critical in writing and development.

Text production instruction should include modeling newly introduced letters, practicing letter names while writing letters, tracing letters with numbered arrow cues, practicing letters from memory, and asking children to circle letters that present their best work. Edwards also points out that handwriting is not just a motor process, but rather draws on the importance of letter recognition (a visual memory skill), which is a skill that can be enhanced by repeated practice with letter production.

Edwards also highlights the importance of *explicit spelling instruction* for kindergarten children and goes on to say that *there are only a limited number of empirical studies regarding how to teach kindergarten children with reading and writing difficulties how to write and highlight future direction for research.*

However, parents should not panic if their child exhibits weak printing or drawing skills. You cannot expect all four-year-olds to ride two wheelers.

Therefore, we should expect the same differences in development with a child's printing or drawing skills. Still, if your child's printing or drawings continue to be delayed and you also notice delays in reading or language development then you might need to have an occupational therapist conduct an evaluation with your child.

Occupational therapists are employed by school districts, county offices of education, and/or privately. An occupational therapist can evaluate your child's sensory-motor development and offer suggestions to address problems before a delay turns into something more serious such as delayed reading and language arts skills.

In the meantime, here are some strategies parents can employ on their own: begin with the basic pencil grip. For example, thick pencils are good for students' little hands and fingers to grip or hold. Furthermore, a child whose pencil grip is claw-like (fingers grip the pencil from the top or at the back of the pencil) places too much stress on the child's weak fingers, which can affect writing skills.

To address the claw-like grip, parents can purchase a pencil grip that works with the body's natural physiology to gently place fingers in the proper position. Also, large lined paper should be the obvious choice, since it offers the child the space to write. Other suggestions could be muscle or finger strengthening by squeezing a rubber ball five to ten times, twice daily or whatever the parent considers the child is capable of achieving.

Again, we must remember that not all children will exhibit the same printing or drawing skills at the outset of their school experience. Still, if the child shows little or no improvement by the beginning of the end of kindergarten or beginning of first grade, then you need to follow some of the suggestions before weak printing and drawing skills can seriously affect future language arts skills, particularly reading.

Chapter 2

Head Start: When a No-Brainer Becomes a Brainer!

President Obama's recent support concerning the importance of early childhood education and/or Head Start is at best a no-brainer. Advertisers have known for years, the sooner you connect with a child's brain, the easier it is to mold. In other words, follow the money and one way or another you will learn that the earlier you stimulate your child's learning brain (learning centers) the greater the learning potential and eventual intelligence.

For example, when three-years-olds were shown photos of different visual advertising icons, the overwhelming icon named was not some children's book character but the McDonald's logo, aka Ronald McDonald, the Golden Arches. This was also evident with the cartoon character Joe Camel of cigarette fame, until some perceptive physician and/or politician made the connection that children cannot discern fact from fiction. The bottom line is that a child's brain can be changed—it is called plasticity.

Evidence of the importance of early brain stimulation can be supported by basic brain physiology. The child's first (brain) growth spurt occurs in utero or when his brain grows to about one pound.

The second growth spurt occurs during the first year of infancy or when another pound is added. Thereafter, the brain will have an extended growth period, from age two to about age fourteen, when another pound is added. The first two brain growth periods are critical to the child's developing brain, indicating why nutrition and early stimulation (touching, bonding, etc.) are so critical to the child's developing brain.

What separates us from other mammals, and gives us a final reprieve, is the third period, or when our mid brain (cognition/emotion) and executive brain develops. It is during this third period when greater nerve density occurs among our billions of neurons. In short, the greater the density, the greater the learning potential, intelligence and again a good reason for Head Start.

Studies have shown the positive impact for three- and four-year-old children enrolled in Head Start on pre-reading, pre-writing, and vocabulary skills. Also discovered was that Head Start parents read more frequently to their children than those parents of children in a control group who were not enrolled in Head Start. In addition, at age three, Head Start children were shown to have larger vocabularies and higher social and emotional development than children in comparable control groups.

An ongoing study was performed in California of more than 600 San Bernardino Head Start graduates. According to a 2003 study, research found that social structures, as a whole, saved nearly $9 for every $1 invested in Head Start. Benefits included increased earnings, employment, and family stability, and decreased welfare dependency, crime, grade repetition, and special education services.

When a child receives early childhood education or Head Start, society is in effect stimulating the child's cognitive/emotional brain (limbic system) or hippocampus (responsible for bonding). And when children develop a positive connection (relationship) to learning and intelligence, they are building a foundation for higher order thinking or the stimulation of our executive brain center.

The executive brain center is associated with higher order thinking, which could have a positive impact on the high school dropout rate (45 to 55 percent), as well as juvenile delinquency. Currently, to educate a high school student costs about $9,000 per year; to incarcerate a juvenile offender the cost is about $85,000 per year (JDI, 2009).

As stated, Head Start is the perfect example of when a no-brainer becomes a brainer.

Chapter 3

Setting the Record Straight About ADHD and Stimulant Medication

A recent article from the CDC (Center for Disease Control Study) concerning the overuse of stimulant medication for ADHD children (two–five) urges parents of preschoolers with ADHD to try *behavior therapy* first before resorting to meds. Behavior therapy encompasses a wide range of interventions from counseling to eight-week boot camps for parents to learn how to better manage difficult behaviors.

Unfortunately, the article fails in some ways to accurately explain the real problem. That is, the CDC study found that 75 percent of preschoolers diagnosed as ADHD are receiving stimulant drugs such as Adderall and Ritalin as treatment. The article adds, *The concern comes from new statistics that show a troubling gap between recommended practices for treating our youngest Americans and what's happening on the ground at doctors' offices.*

Further, the CDC recommends that parents of ADHD children try behavior therapy first, but less than half are receiving such services. For example, ISMP (Institute of Safe Medication Practices) identified additional drugs that accounted for 41 percent of serious adverse events in children due to drug medications reported to the US Food and Drug Administration between 2008 and 2012.

One study identified 45,610 adverse drug effects reported in children less than eighteen years of age. Of these, 64 percent (29,298) indicated serious injury. Reports of children suffering from abuse of such medications grew in time from 6,320 in 2008 to 11,401 in 2012 increasing at the same rate as for adult patients (ISMP—2014). Along with Adderall and Ritalin, the list included Concerta, Atomoxetine, and Strattera.

Notable negative effects showed suicidal behavior, aggression and hallucinations or other manifestations of psychosis. Cardiac arrest was associated with methylphenidate, and weight loss or arrested growth was also reported for Concerta, Atomoxetine, and Strattera (ISMP—2014).

The question that needs to be asked: why were only Ritalin and Adderall cited among the drugs when other drugs are also being abused? Further, why identify only children ages two to five as at risk when the medication negatively affects the brains of eighteen-year-olds also?

Further, CDC mentions the most recent US guidelines, issued by the APA in 2011. These guidelines present a movement toward nonmedical interventions about the potential benefits of parent or teacher directed behavior therapy as the first line of treatment. The CDC states: *"Only if that therapy does not provide significant improvement or the child has moderate or severe symptoms should MDs prescribe medications."*

Also troubling is that although the CDC study recommends *behavior therapy* as the *number one alternative* supported by the American Pediatric Association, it fails to mention specifically that the American Pediatric Association recommends neurofeedback as the number one alternative to medication for ADHD children (APA, 2011). Neurofeedback is a brain-training program that has proven to be successful with ADHD children, as well as RAD and PTSD clients. Interestingly, the article fails to mention that the rise of ADHD diagnoses and prescriptions for stimulants coincided with a remarkably successful two-decade campaign by pharmaceutical companies to publicize ADHD and promote the pills to doctors, educators, and parents.

With the children's market booming, the industry is now employing similar marketing techniques as it focuses on adult ADHD, which could become even more profitable. Sales of prescription stimulants have more than quintupled from two billion dollars in 2002 to eight billion dollars in 2014 (Schwarz, A Health—2014).

Perhaps one reason why the CDC didn't address the eighteen and under age group and focused only two- to five-year-old age group would be the cost to insurance companies and the medical establishments. You decide.

Chapter 4

Increasing Reading Fluency with Beginning Readers

One of the most difficult challenges parents face with reading is how to increase reading fluency with their beginning reader. For example, low reading fluency can actually be traced to the learning style of your child. In other words, children defined as verbal learners often have an easier time with fluency because they have the ability to think part to whole and either sight-read or learn to decode reading words. The ability to decode supports increased reading fluency, as well as reading comprehension, because increased reading vocabulary feeds into the meaning of the word or story.

Another group of children are those defined as visual or nonverbal learners, such as children who see words as whole to part and attempt to sight-read rather than to decode words. Children in this group who try to sight-read rather than break the words up into parts fall behind with fluency because half of the English words are made up of silent letters.

If a child cannot sight-read, he needs to decode to understand meaning, which again, leads to greater fluency and comprehension. Unfortunately for such children, reading fluency becomes an even greater struggle, particularly after third grade, the level at which the learner is expected to become an independent reader. That is, children in these intermediate grades will be required to read longer, more difficult passages; fluency at this point becomes imperative to school success.

Further, children who only *word call* or decode words individually without connecting them together for meaning face an uphill battle because the more rapidly the child reads, the greater the reading comprehension. Regardless of your child's particular learning style, teachers and parents can take the lead with various strategies to ensure greater confidence and self-motivation to read.

One strategy is called *rehearsal*, a reading by a parent with his child of high frequency words such as the *Dolce Reading List*. My suggestion is that you post on a white board any words that are missed and use them for spelling lists, as well as for flash cards, for practice. After these *high frequency words* are mastered, children can increase their reading fluency.

Another strategy is called *pre-reading*. Parent and child should look at the title of a new story and try to guess what the story is about. Next, they can think of words that the author might use in writing the story. Finally, help the child to begin to think about words in the text that will give him practice in dealing with more difficult words for future reading exercises.

A highly successful reading strategy is called *Echo Reading*, which addresses fluency through repetition and practice, and builds confidence. With echo reading the parent reads a sentence and the child echoes the reading, eventually reading the selection with the same expression as they are hearing. This can be achieved from *The Big Book Reading Series* St. Louis, Mo. (Book Source, 2017); along the same line is *choral reading*, which suggests reading in small groups of children, reading continually in unison, using each other's voices to stay fluent.

The *Read Aloud Program* is an excellent strategy for parents to stimulate reading fluency. It simply asks parents to read one story to their child, three times per week in twenty-minute intervals. Success rates of the 100 plus Read Aloud experimental programs showed a 50 percent increase in participating children's voluntary reading time and interest.

Implementing these strategies with oral reading of articles and time for rehearsal and practice helps comprehension, sight vocabulary, and reading confidence.

Moreover, combining fluency within the context of a complete reading program has been shown to stimulate greater interest, especially among struggling readers and gives them the needed support to become independent readers.

Chapter 5

It's OK for Children to Fantasize About Their Intelligence

A major connection between fantasy and intelligence begins in early childhood or as early as three years of age. For example, during this period, the children's intelligence is centered on one idea and that is their own wellbeing, getting their needs met. Due to this developmental stage, children can focus passionately on Santa Claus, the Easter Bunny, etc.

And it does not matter if older brother or sister has *spilled the beans* that Santa Claus is a fake. Again, at this age, fantasy is very real, and it will not be given up until about age six or seven when their brains are able to entertain more than one idea at a time or Santa Claus is actually daddy or a stand-in mom. The moral of the story? Although they know Santa is not real, they do know that you still get presents; so, they are smart enough to go with the flow.

Moreover, when fantasy is connected to intelligence, the experience is not only very powerful and passionate, but the experience of fantasy can also become cemented in their brains for the long term. For example, when individuals carry some childhood fantasy into adulthood, particularly when it can be connected vocationally, they are often very successful.

At age six, successful talk show host Johnny Carson's fantasy was to become a magician. He asked and received from his parents a book about how to perform magic tricks. Buried under his fantasy of becoming a magician was a very shy child who would use magic as a scaffold for confidence, allowing him to stand up in front of an audience and perform magic tricks. The end result was one of the most successful late night talk show hosts whose fantasy to perform magic became the ability to perform verbal tricks in front of millions of TV viewers!

Furthermore, between the ages of seven and ten fantasy becomes even more important because the child can now entertain two ideas at a time—himself and the skills that allow him to act out his fantasy. This is a critical time when the child's fantasy is connected to his intelligence. More importantly, at this age, the window is beginning to close and fantasies often become less passionate as we experience challenges and failures. So why not feed the fantasy while they are still free of all the baggage?

During these periods Johnny Carson was not just doing magic tricks for his family, he was now taking his act out into the neighborhood, expanding his fantasy and intelligence for greater things to come.

The third and final stage of fantasy and intelligence, ages eleven and older, is more abstract and tells us what came next for Johnny Carson and his magic act. At this stage he had the ability to entertain more than three plus ideas at a time. Now, fantasy and intelligence moves beyond simply skill development to the abstract field of other possibilities. For Carson, it was larger groups but with additional components—notoriety and financial success.

Carson went to a university, got a degree in communication, worked college radio, and after graduation, moved to host television game shows. He moved up the TV ladder until he got the *Tonight Show* and metaphorically became a magician in his ability to entertain audiences for many years!

When the young child fantasizes, he is beginning to connect with the pure intelligence of childhood. It is often free of ego and the baggage of failure. Therefore, a word to the wise—when your child expresses a fantasy, particularly about a vocation, listen intensely and then see what magic can come from it. If Carson were alive today, he might echo the same belief.

Chapter 6

Television and the Developing Brain

A good example of pioneer TV programing and children's brain development is the popular PBS children's show *Sesame Street*, particularly its role in stimulating language development. In fact, the *Sesame Street* producers smartly surmised that effective children's TV programing that focused on the areas of the brain responsible for language development could advance children's expressive language.

Studies show that children who watch *Sesame Street* at age two score higher on school readiness tests in kindergarten than those who do not. Another study found that frequent *Sesame Street* viewing in preschool is associated with higher grade point averages in high school or almost 16 percent higher than those children who didn't grow up watching the program (Fisch & Truglio, 2001). Further, children who watch *Sesame Street* episodes that had positive social messages showed much higher levels of positive social behavior than those children who did not watch *Sesame Street* (*The Atlantic*, 2015).

Other TV programing suggests similar improvements with children's language development. For example, at thirty months of age, watching *Dora the Explorer*, *Blue's Clues*, *Arthur*, *Clifford*, or *Dragon Tales* resulted in greater vocabularies and higher expressive language scores; watching *Teletubbies* was related to fewer vocabulary words and smaller expressive language scores; and viewing *Barney & Friends* was related to fewer vocabulary words and more expressive language (American Behavioral Scientist, January 2005).

For instance, one area of the brain crucial to language and reading development has to do with *working memory*. During a reading exercise, working memory is the amount of time the child's brain processes the visual and auditory representations of letters and words. When the child's visual brain processes faster than the auditory or vice versa is when learning to read becomes a challenge. Fortunately, as the child's brain matures so does his ability to coordinate these two critical language areas and reading ceases to become a chore. Working memory was probably one of the major areas that *Sesame Street* had in mind when their programing was created.

In addition, it was no coincidence that *Sesame Street* was based on the popular adult TV show *Laugh In*. *Laugh In* like *Sesame Street* presented short bursts of information, which is how working memory effectively operates. With *Laugh In* it was with short jokes. With *Sesame Street* it was with letters and words laced with phonics, etc.

Moreover, another important area of language development is how important the child's kinesthetic intelligence is utilized in the *Sesame Street*'s format, especially how it is related to reading and the child's *cerebellum*.

At one time, the cerebellum, located in the lower area of the brain, was believed to be solely responsible for motor skills or movement. However, brain scientists and astute reading specialists now realize that the cerebellum is critical for reading mastery because it connects the occipital (visual), the auditory (temporal) with the sensory motor (somatosensory cortex) brain areas. or the executive brain areas.

Furthermore, addressing the cerebellum was one reason why *Sesame Street* uses song, dance, and children framing the letters of the alphabet or phonics with their bodies as an effective strategy to teach language development, as well as reading.

Also, how *Sesame Street* used puppets (Oscar the Grouch) to teach language development while interacting with humans is a thing of beauty. This approach further stimulated the magical child's brain (two- to six-year-old), which is linked to the child's emotional brain or limbic system. Once the child's brain formed a *relationship* to the emotional aspects of learning, greater language development could become a foundation for greater language development, as well as higher reading potential.

The question needs to be asked is why successful children's TV programs is still only a blimp on the radar of TV programming and children's brain development? Why do some parents (still) allow their children's brains to be exposed to long periods of commercial TV programing when the success of commercial TV shows has been documented *not* to improve children's brain development? Maybe this is why Oscar became a grouch?

Chapter 7

Overprotective Parents—Give Me a Break!

With the school year coming to a close and summer vacation upon us, it is a troubling time for all parents, particularly for *overprotective parents*. Children will now come in contact with an expansion of territory. From water to biking and even computer use, parents will need to find balance with boundaries and rules. According to author, Hanna Rosin, *overprotective behavior of modern parents is destroying children's independence, trapping them in a hyper-controlled bubble that they might never escape.*

For example, overprotective parents limit risk-taking and make kids fearful of attempting new experiences. Rosin cites research out of Norway that shows that kids' brains are programmed evolutionarily to be *risk-takers in order to survive*. That is, kids who take risks tend to be less fearful, more independent adults, and kids who don't take risks, end up on the sidelines of life.

Dr. Ellen Sangster who studied the effects of risk-taking in young kids says, *"Our fear of children being harmed . . . may result in more fearful children and increased levels of psychopathology, . . . things like climbing, wrestling and exploring alone are essential in helping kids conquer small challenges so they can prepare for bigger ones."*

Furthermore, as insidious as it is to protect kids from taking risks, another sidenote to overprotective parents is the fact that they prevent kids from experiencing failure. In school, sports, playgroups, when their child fails, it is often the school's or teacher's fault. In playgroups it is always the other child who is at fault.

Overprotective parents can actually affect a child's brain development. For example, such children will often not bond with social or academic situations. The inability to bond is associated with a part of the brain called the limbic system. That is, children who fail to bond in various situations often take a *fight or flight* response to new situations. This inability prevents the child

15

from bonding with new experiences and challenges, which can seriously affect the brain's hippocampus.

The hippocampus is responsible for bonding and attaches to higher order thinking and the executive centers of the brain. The lack of the development of the ability to use our higher centers of the brain and actually think out of the box could block evolutionary thinking of such children.

Moreover, parents need to understand that their overprotection can begin early in the child's life or the first few weeks of infancy. The late Dr. Margaret Mahler coined this period *separation and individuation.*

Mahler theorized that after the first few weeks of infancy, in which the infant is either sleeping or barely conscious, the infant progresses first from a phase (normal-symbiotic phase) in which it perceives itself as one with its mother within the larger environment to an extended phase (separation-individuation phase) consisting of several stages or sub-phases in which the infant slowly comes to distinguish itself from its mother, and then, by degrees, discovers its own identity, will, and individuality. It is this time when parents must pull back and allow the child to begin to experience his power through separation and establish his so-called own individuality.

Psychologist Erick Erickson's two early childhood stages would be antithetical to overprotective parents. His first stage is defined as autonomy versus doubt and shame (ages eighteen months to three years) followed by initiative versus guilt (ages three to five years). These two stages, along with Mahler's individuation and separation stage, are essentially periods of the child's life when overprotective parents could be setting a course of doubt, shame, guilt, and failure for their children.

Chapter 8

Teaching RAD (Reactive Attachment Disorder) Students

Teachers need support in teaching RAD (reactive attachment disorder) students. We hear a great deal about ADHD children and failed school performance but ironically very little is said about RAD students. RAD students exhibit serious social/emotional issues, which makes them view every new learning situation, every new relationship with mistrust and fear.

The angry or seriously withdrawn student who disrespects you at every step is in reality a very frightened child trying to survive. In short, RAD students have serious abandonment issues caused by a separation from their caregivers that are often compared to a *paper cut* to the heart that never heals. Like a bottomless pail that flows out, teachers can never stop trying to reach this child due to the RAD students' mistrustful personalities.

For example, a major area of the brain located in the limbic system is the thalamus, which interprets danger and threats to our survival. When the brain interprets the world with extreme mistrust the thalamus sends a signal to another part of the limbic system called the amygdala and a fight or flight response ensues.

Adoptive and/or abused children are prime candidates for attachment disorders and almost always link even the most unthreatening experience to their survival. The umbilical cord that connects them with their caregivers has been severed. To make matters worse the chemical cortisol gives their brain a jolt to fight or flight, which only exacerbates the interpretation.

School and its learning environment is such a threat to RAD students because education can be a predominantly left-brain exercise or linear, sequential, mathematical processing. For many RAD students, the *Catch-22* is that the right side of their brain, (nonlinear side) becomes dominant or on fire. These are students who will excel in art, but anything verbal, logical, mathematical becomes a test of survival. Conversely, securely attached students do not have this problem. Securely attached students signal to the thalamus that they trust school, learning and teachers.

The hippocampus, the seat of emotional relationships, also located in the limbic system, bonds with learning and moves those processes to the higher centers of the brain for an optimal learning experience. RAD students' brains mistrust this left-brain learning experience unless it is something kinesthetic, visual and/or associated with the arts. Again, it is for this reason that RAD students are often gifted artistically or kinesthetically.

Since many RAD students suffer academically, teachers will be more successful with RAD students if they combine lessons that are visual or kinesthetic with remediation. (Please see *The Promised Cookie: No Longer Angry Children*—Author House, 2011). I successfully employed a curriculum that was artistic and kinesthetic to reach my RAD students. For example, to teach writing, teachers had RAD students first illustrate the writing experience which then became a book. Writing their own books was used to reinforce fluency by having them attach words to their illustrations.

In addition, they used their books to read to younger children, further reinforcing the learning or bonding experience.

Choral Reading was also effective because it allowed the students to read along with their teachers, reinforcing the bonding process. Moreover, teachers always had the students begin every reading exercise by first interpreting illustrations. Math remediation was also supported artistically and kinesthetically. Students measured and drew the school's building and grounds and then incorporated the measurements into the diagrams of the buildings. Also, students created balsa wood models of the school's building and grounds for further bonding.

Finally, teachers incorporated an individualized math program that allowed the students to graph their progress. The graphs served as another visual reinforcement when they were displayed on the classroom walls. Furthermore, the math program provided students with an immediate reinforcement because the answers were located on the side of each page. After they completed the examples, they could turn to the answers for immediate reinforcement and empowerment.

When teaching RAD students, remember that their true genius and safety is the visual or right side of their brains. If you want to connect with the left side you must first *put the fire out* on the right side.

Chapter 9

Learning How to Remember

All students at some time in their school lives will need to *learn strategies about how to remember* some lesson or homework activity regardless of their interest level. For some students this is a problem, not because they lack the intelligence but because their brains often reject learning what they term as *boring information*.

Instead, many students are literally *thrown to the wolves* without teaching them proven strategies to soften the difficulties associated with having to learn new information. Strategies are critical because they eliminate the student from blocking; they can't recall information even after hours of studying!

Moreover, learning how-to-remember strategies would certainly help parents from pulling their hair out every time the student is required to study for a spelling test or learn the fifty states and capitals. As much as parents and students rail against certain assignments, such lessons will always be a part of school and in some ways, however good or bad, only expose the student's inability to use strategies about how they remember.

Finally, we should thank teachers for assigning such exercises because learning math facts or states and capitals can be an essential foundation for future learning experiences.

With this in mind, let's look at what researchers theorize how and what students learn to remember best. (Note to reader: we must remember that students exhibit strengths in different intelligences or learning styles. Students who are verbally gifted could experience greater learning in lectures, while for students who might learn best visually, their learning could be higher when watching movies or viewing a slide lecture, etc.)

Most students only remember about 10 percent of what they read, and this is lowered if they are disinterested or begin to move around shortly thereafter.

Next is what they hear, or about 20 percent, and this also is lowered if their listening lacks any emotional connection to the subject for discussion; 30 percent of what they see, such as looking at pictures or photos; 40 percent, as in watching a movie, but again, this could rise if the film is interesting; 50 percent, such as looking at an exhibit that is appealing; 70 to 80 percent, as in participating in a discussion about something they care about, such as giving a talk, doing a dramatic presentation, or simulating a real experience. Lastly, a high of 90 percent of what they prefer to say and do.

Notice the words *prefer to say and do*, which would obviously be supportive of personal interests. Again, these percentages should not be generalized to the entire school age population, only that some students' learning-to-remember skills are less developed than others.

In short, notice how the percentages tend to parallel or connect with certain learning theories, such as Howard Gardner's theory of multiple intelligence: *children learn best when we recognize their preferred intelligences.*

Moreover, children who demonstrate a high linguistic intelligence or good verbal skills could expect to remember 90 percent of what they read or children who exhibit strong visual or spatial intelligence could remember 90 percent of what they see.

There are many concrete strategies to help your student to learn to remember all types of information such as *chunking* or *grouping* information according to what they have in common; also, deep processing or relating the material to themselves; organizing through meaning and association, such as pairing it with something they know very well. Also, active learning or attending to what they are learning; visual memory, such as diagrams, tables, outlines, and graphs.

Furthermore, talking it out, as in verbally reciting the information aloud, and finally visualizing or presenting as in teaching the material are other strategies.

Therefore, the wise parent or teacher needs not only to learn strategies that will help the student's learning to remember ability, but also to be aware of how children learn and express their intelligence as in learning styles or multiple intelligence theories.

Chapter 10

The Power of Children's Intelligence

Every child should have the opportunity to experience the power of his multiple intelligence and learning potential. (And the sooner the better!) Tapping into one's preferred intelligence is nothing more than identifying any one of the *eight intelligences* defined by Howard Gardner's theory of multiple intelligence.

When children experience the power of their so-called *preferred intelligence*, they often begin to transfer this power or feeling to other learning situations. Some children exhibit their preferred intelligence visually, others verbally and still others kinesthetically. The key is that when they attach their so-called preferred intelligence to learning potential children will begin to feel the real power of their intelligence, and learning could cease to be a struggle.

Dr. Maria Montessori saw the connection in the power of multiple intelligence and learning potential with orphaned children. She recognized this dilemma by creating a school or learning environment based on stimulating the child's kinesthetic intelligence. In effect, she was sublimating the lack of a mother's touch through the use of manipulatives. For example, to teach the alphabet, she created sandpaper letters so her students could trace their fingers over the letter to stimulate greater brain development, as well as linguistic skills.

Perceptive teachers and parents recognize differences in children's intelligence and learning styles and attach play or emotional involvement (fun) with cognition or learning as a technique to expose their children to successful learning situations or intelligences. Again, Montessori took this approach to another level due to the severe backgrounds of her student population.

Moreover, when children are allowed to attach their preferred intelligence with their learning potential, they often make an easier transition to other learning situations, particularly in skill development. An excellent example of this are the cases of unsuccessful students who finally find success in the world and branch into other previously unavailable skills after having had a period of success in their vocation of choice. Unfortunately, for some children, the later they experience the power of their preferred intelligence, the more difficult it is for them to succeed in school and, in general, deal with life's many challenges.

Sometimes it takes luck, perseverance, a perceptive parent or teacher to help the children or adults connect with their particular learning style or multiple intelligence. For some individuals, it may never happen. Tragically, those people never fulfill the power of their multiple intelligence or learning brain and struggle through life. We often refer to such individuals as *underachievers*.

Further, child specialists often see great variations in their academic successes and failures. Some children experience homework success, but fail on tests. Others perform poorly on homework and do well on tests. The variations or ups and downs can be linked to the child's inability to connect his preferred intelligence and learning brain to other learning modalities such as used in math or science.

For example, it is assumed that children who demonstrate a high kinesthetic intelligence automatically do well in sports. However, such children can also do well in math and science by using hands-on experiments to feed into this power. Rumor had it that Albert Einstein developed his scientific theory of relativity kinesthetically or with his body.

Whatever the case, the more the child is allowed to experience the power of his multiple intelligence, the easier it is for him to connect or combine this ability into skill development, and hopefully the ups and downs of learning, school performance, and life's challenges will not be so pronounced.

Chapter 11

Boys Will Be Boys!

Developmental differences among students can affect school performance, particularly with mandated curriculums, testing pressures, etc. Combine these differences with a shortened school year, larger class sizes, fewer support services and we can recognize a few causes of poor male student performance.

Another factor rarely discussed, but known by brain researchers is that reading and/or language arts skills *are not natural* learning paradigms for boys' brains. In other words, we need to recognize that the brains of the male gender are structured differently from that of the female gender, which generally does well in reading and language arts.

Brain differences not only affect a boy's linguistic abilities (reading, writing, etc.) but also affect his social development. The corpus callosum, a part of the brain that serves as a bridge between our brain's right and left hemispheres is smaller in boys than in girls. The 25 percent difference in size causes less communication between the two halves for the male gender, diminishing cross talking and multitasking, which support increased language arts skills.

Further, the hippocampus, a major component for memory storage, is smaller in boys, than in girls. As a result, boys learn to read nine months later than girls, and the average boy's learning capacity for writing and formation of words is also nine to twelve months later for boys than for girls (USDE, 2008)!

Moreover, the prefrontal cortex, seat of executive function, and a part of the brain responsible for decision making, organization, abstract thinking is more developed in girls than in boys. Additional statistics indicate that boys, ages five to twelve, are more likely than girls to have repeated one grade; 42 percent of boys have been suspended once by age seventeen; only 65 percent of boys graduate from high school, compared to 72 percent of girls.

Finally, the amygdala, a part of the brain that signals fight or flight is larger and faster growing in boys than in girls, which could be a reason why boys are 2.5 times more likely to be diagnosed as ADHD (USDE, 2008).

The following are some recommendations and effective strategies for teachers and schools in response to the needs of the male gender: vary teaching strategies, especially in the language arts; use symbols, abstractions, diagrams, objects in space, as well as technology and manipulatives.

Boys have more spatial and mechanical functioning, which supports more hands-on learning experiences for boys. Also, enlist male mentors for male students. Only one out of every nine teachers are males in this country, and the United States leads the industrial world in the percentage of *fatherless* boys.

What can schools do to support these statistics? Some public schools now offer single sex classrooms in order to allow both genders to be more focused on studies. The Gates Foundation is now setting goals of reforming high school curriculums to help male students benefit from this mission of more flexibility in teaching approaches. Currently, the Gurian Institute has trained more than 60,000 teachers as to how to work more effectively with male students (Gurian Institute, 2015).

Chapter 12

Delayed Gratification and School Success

A Stanford University study (1972) was interested in finding out if one group of six-year-olds could wait for a reward (delayed gratification). That is, would they be more successful in life than children who could not wait for an additional reward. The experimenters presented each child with a marshmallow, which they could eat immediately. Or, if they could wait fifteen minutes they would get two marshmallows.

The psychologists followed both groups over a lengthy number of years and found that the children who were willing to delay gratification and waited to receive the second marshmallow ended up having higher SAT scores, lower levels of substance abuse, lower likelihood of obesity, better responses to stress, better social skills as reported by their parents, and generally better scores in a range of other life measures.

Perhaps those children who expressed a so-called weakness in their inability to delay gratification also had difficulty in other cognitive areas?

In addition, certain attributes are essential for future executive functioning such as greater attention span; who or what you have just seen or heard is retrievable from working memory and especially delayed gratification. In short, these capabilities may predict success in school and even in the working world.

Fortunately brain scientists believe that executive functioning can be teachable. For example, one educational curriculum called *Tools of the Mind* has had success in some low-income school districts when compared to children from high-income districts. The program trains kids to revisit temptation and distraction and to practice tasks designed to enhance working memory and flexible thinking. Examples of self-regulation tasks are simply teaching children to tell themselves aloud what to do (Stix, 2015).

Other successful approaches to produce cognition (delayed gratification) have allied itself with music rather than computer games that claim to boost memory, etc. Some of the research findings come from a group of neuroscientists led by Nin Kraus of Northwestern University. Kraus is head of the Auditory Neuroscience Laboratory. She used EEG (electroencephalograph) recordings to measure if practicing music can improve cognitive faculties.

Her lab has found that such training enhances *working memory*, and perhaps most important, makes students better listeners, allowing them to subtract speech from the-all-talking-at-once that sometimes prevails in the classroom. Kraus has worked with the *Harmony Project* and published a study in 2014 that showed in one of its programs that children who practiced a musical instrument could process sounds closely linked to reading and language skills better than children who only did so for a year (Stix, 2015).

Music training's impact extends even to academic classes. The *Harmony Project* provides music education to lower income youngsters in Los Angeles schools. Dozens of students participating in the project have graduated from high school and gone to college, usually the first in their family to do so.

According to Krus, *"If students have to choose how to spend their time between computer games or a musical instrument, there is no question, in my mind, which one is more beneficial for the nervous system. If you are trying to copy a guitar lead, you have to keep it in your head and try to reproduce it over and over."*

Chapter 13

Giving Voice to Their Grief

Counselors and psychologists must now address an unspeakable tragedy and begin the healing process with the Newtown, Connecticut, children. Experienced counselors and psychologists will do their best to heal but their role will be extremely difficult. One of the many problems they face will be the addressing of the different emotional and/or cognitive developmental levels of the children they counsel.

Young children have different levels in how they express themselves emotionally and cognitively, particularly in how they deal with grief and death. Some children are more verbal and feel comfortable speaking to adults about grief, while others are non verbal and will internalize their grief. The key factor in the success of the counseling is the approach the counselor uses to address the children's pain or grief.

For example, most experienced counselors understand these differences which is why they use different modes of therapy to reach individuals, especially young children dealing with the extreme tragedy of death. Fortunately, many grief counselors use the expressive arts, such as art therapy as their main strategy for helping children deal with the often-unspeakable thoughts and/or emotions associated with death.

According to art therapist Mary Gambarony of the Riverview Medical Center: *"Whether it's drawing, painting, sculpture or any other medium, it's always been a powerful way to express emotions without words. It allows children to take the pain and to take the sadness, take the frustration, take the questions, and put it outside of themselves and that's very healing in itself to get it out of you, and put it outside of themselves and that's very healing in itself to get it out of you, put it on something objective in front of you and be able to look at it."* She adds, *"regardless of its presentation, they're all symbols of loss and pain that children often have trouble expressing. The art gives voice to their grief."*

What is often not discussed are the causes of this healing process and the continued need for expressive arts or art therapy in grief counseling, especially with children.

Art can stimulate multiple areas of the brain, particularly when one is attempting to heal a child's psyche associated with a major tragedy such as death. When a counselor attempts to help a child speak about a tragedy, he often focuses only on the verbal or linguistic areas of the brain, which can negate those children whose cognitive processes are more non verbal. Conversely, forcing only the non verbal expression does not address the needs of children who can be verbally expressive. Even for the verbal child, discussion does not lead to expressing the depth of grief, while an artistic expression can often allow the experience.

The effectiveness of art therapy is that it addresses both sides of the brain or the child's verbal or non verbal intelligences and emotions. This is particularly true with the right side of the brain, considered our visual and more emotional side. Although we use both sides of our brain simultaneously, some children (especially girls) have an edge because the corpus callosum, a strip that runs down the center of the brain is larger in girls, which allows the two halves of the brain to cross talk, an indication of why art therapy can be so effective for girls.

For boys, whose corpus callosum is smaller, they do not have the luxury of being able to cross talk as effectively. However, art therapy can specifically stimulate the right side or visual—emotional side of the boy's brain, which allows for the grief to be looked at openly, thus giving voice to his grief.

Whatever expressive arts a counselor chooses in dealing with a child's grief, the key is to understand that beyond the different developmental levels of a child's grieving emotions, there are major factors involved in the healing process that go beyond simply talking about a tragic experience. The brain is far more complex, and as such, needs expressive forms of therapy that will address multiple areas of the brain for the unspeakable and/or speakable wound to be healed.

Chapter 14

When IQ Tests Take Precedent over True Intelligence

Recently, a psychologist friend received a call from a parent who requested that he conduct an IQ assessment with her six-year-old daughter. His response was as follows: "*First and foremost, I do not prescribe labeling or attaching an IQ score to any particular child, let alone a 11-year-old, for the simple reason that the limiting effects of labeling often outweigh the productive results.*"

IQ tests, more often than not, *can* stigmatize the child's intellectual potential. Furthermore, the IQ score often disregards the factor of the child's emotional state associated with a test-taking situation, regardless of how skillful the tester or how *unbiased* the environment.

Moreover, attaching a number to a child's name can change the mindset of parents and educators about a child's learning potential. Rosenthal and Jacobson, in their 1968 study on the effects of teacher expectancies, found results that place an enormous emphasis on the role of a teacher. Their study describes that within each of eighteen classrooms, an average of 20 percent of the children were reported to classroom teachers as showing unusual potential for intellectual gains. Eight months later these *unusual children* (who had actually been selected at random) showed significantly greater gains in IQ than did the remaining children in the group defined as *simply intelligent*.

The following is a specific example of the lack of validity of IQ tests. Larry P. was a young African American child who was diagnosed as having *educable mental retardation (EMR)*, and as a result, he received educational services in a self-contained EMR classroom. The sole criterion for the eligibility into the EMR program was an IQ test result. *Larry P. vs. Riles* was a class action case that questioned the validity of placing young black children into special education classes solely on the basis of an IQ test.

The case argued that the tests were culturally discriminatory against black children who were placed in EMR classrooms. From 1968 until the trial in 1977, black children were overly represented in EMR classrooms, particularly since in1968–1969 black children made up about 9 percent of the school population but 27 percent were reported in EMR classrooms. The court held that the IQ tests were *culturally biased* against black children and banned the CA school system from using IQ tests to place black children in special education classes. Today the courts require a more extensive approach to identifying *all* children in special education classes.

IQ tests are often perceived as a challenge to a child's intelligence. Regardless of the tester's ability, the emotional make-up of the child can never be perfectly determined. Brain scientists know that when the child *feels safe* and/or does not *feel threatened* in a testing situation, the child's brain potential (usually) responds more favorably. However, when the child feels threatened, which can occur in an intelligence-testing situation, the child's brain responds in a fight or flight response, reducing brain potential. The negative effects of IQ testing far outweigh the pluses. You decide.

Chapter 15

Developmental Delays and School Readiness

Educational specialists often speak about developmental delays or how age and not just ability determines a student's readiness for learning. Combine this with mandated tests, state standards and uncertain home support and teachers often are faced with the perfect storm called student failure. For example, Remer (1976) tested K-12 students and found that in most classrooms there are usually two and three developmental learning levels or how students' learn and acquire information.

Researchers found that 65 to 70 percent of high school seniors *never reach* formal operational or abstract thinking, generally considered the highest level of cognitive development (Lawson & Wollman, 1976). Formal operational thinking begins to kick in as early as age eleven, when children are expected to entertain three plus operations at a time (long division) and full formal about age fourteen (algebra).

Not addressing developmental delays associated with learning is a little like expecting all four-year-olds to ride two wheelers or expecting all nine- and ten-year-olds to do long division—which requires knowledge of 1 through 12 math facts and four division operations. Teachers understand and struggle with developmental delays all the time using various remediation techniques to deal with their student developmental levels.

One key to addressing this issue could begin at home with parents who need to understand how developmental delays can affect their child's ability to learn. For example, a first grader's homework assignment is to read one story. Parent and child read one story, but they have fifteen minutes left before bedtime. The parent suggests they read another story, but the child refuses because *teacher said to read only one story!* The mother might view the child's response as disobedient, even lazy, but in reality the child is only responding at a developmental level, or how most seven-year-olds think, which is the ability to entertain (only) one perspective at a time, which in this case is the teacher.

In less than a year the same child will be more mature or have the capacity to entertain two ideas at one time, such as teacher and parent. In the future when the mother suggests they read another story and the child understands and agrees. The end result is a positive learning experience or something the parent and child can build upon for future learning situations?

The second area is remediation, or how do teachers raise children's developmental learning levels so they can keep up with the classroom lessons? For instance, I presented the example of fourth graders who were asked to classify five animals (duck, dog, elephant, eagle, and bat) into groups. The majority of the fourth graders classified the animals concretely or walking and flying or four legs and two legs. However, there was a small segment of students who reasoned at formal operational thinking and recognized that bats are mammals and not birds, or that bats are a species of mammals that also fly.

When the teacher tested the same class, a small percentage still grouped the animals concretely or *walking and flying*. The teacher solved this problem by bringing in a live bat so the children could make a personal learning connection. The next time the students were tested they successfully grouped the animals according to species.

Teachers almost always use many strategies to remediate developmental delays, which in this case was to have the class visually experience a live bat! Whatever the case we must continue to educate parents about developmental delays, and always remember our example that all four-year-olds should not be expected to ride two wheelers. When they cannot, they need training wheels, like bringing into the classroom a live bat to increase student learning and even intelligence.

Section II

LATE CHILDHOOD

Figure 2.1
istock.com/FatCamera

AGES SEVEN TO TEN

Kids don't remember what you try to teach them. They remember what you are.

—Jim Henson

Late childhood, the seven- to eleven-year-old developmental stage, is often a mixed blessing for parents and teachers. Children at this stage tend to look at the world in black and white and can think about two ideas at one time. *You scratch my back, I will scratch yours* is their motto for dealing with friends and parents.

We must remember that at this age they are directed toward satisfying their own needs and occasionally others. Their relationships are actually viewed like a marketplace: *What can I get without giving up too much of myself?* They can display fairness and even equal sharing, unfortunately, a sense of loyalty and gratitude is often lacking.

The key to reaching children at this stage is helping them learn to be empathetic and kind to others, while still respecting their need for fairness. School programs that integrate the arts with the academics provide excellent opportunities for children at this stage. The key is to attach their emotions with the academics under the guise of art or creative activities, which makes the school experience actually *fair* and reinforces developmental psychologist Erik Erikson's psychosocial stage (Industry vs. Inferiority) of being industrious instead of inferior.

No school curriculum is perfect or matches-up with the child's cognitive or learning brain. However, it is critical that we always keep our eye on the ball as to where we want to go with this child's learning brain. Our school curriculums are highly developmental and as such, so should the child's social and moral development be as well.

The old saying that children would never learn rules to games if they didn't have fun playing the game seems to describe the premise of *fair versus unfair* perfectly.

Chapter 16

Non-Readers Read Between the Lines

From time to time teachers are faced with students who are defined as non-readers—students who literally do not like to read! The non-reader usually becomes apparent around middle school and continues through high school and beyond with the same aversion to the written word. For some students it could be poor skill development traced to their early primary years, causing reading to become a constant challenge.

For other students, who have good fluency and reading comprehension, reading becomes a struggle with physically remaining focused. This inability to focus often is confused with disinterest. It is this latter group that is the most problematic and frustrating for teachers and parents.

The teacher's first step toward reaching any non-reader should be to conduct a reading assessment to determine if the student indeed has a learning disability that is affecting his non-reading status. If the student shows no reading disability, the teacher could conduct a multiple intelligence assessment (Please see H. Gardner's eight types of multiple intelligence) to determine interest or their multiple intelligence.

Once the teacher can determine the student's multiple intelligence, he or she could recommend specific reading material that connects with the student's specific interest and/or intelligence. For example, teachers often see parallels between students who demonstrate strengths in kinesthetic intelligence and those who become non-readers. This group excels when they are able to use their bodies to express their intelligence. Sitting for thirty minutes reading anything is actually difficult for this group. They would rather be up and moving, building something with their hands rather than reading.

One approach would be for the teacher to find magazines that attempts to link the student's kinesthetic intelligence with skateboarding, basketball, snowboarding, etc. The magazine could stimulate such students to read brief accounts of high interest (photos, etc.) containing information that may neutralize their energetic bodies, allowing them to sit for longer periods of time.

If the teacher has spurred the student's intelligence with magazines, their next step is to find biographies of successful individuals that are attached to their intelligences, such as Tony Hawk with skateboarding, Shaun White with snowboarding, Michael Jordan with basketball, etc.

Another teaching strategy teachers can employ is less scientific, but can actually help define a non-reader's multiple intelligence. Your student loves baseball. Although he has good reading skills, he is still failing miserably in school because he hates to read. After the first meeting, the teacher asks the student to choose one of two books and read only one chapter. The two base-ball books were *Money Ball* by Michael Lewis and *Men at Work* by George Will.

The teacher believes that either book could certainly stimulate this non-reader who loves baseball. In addition, the teacher assumes that if the student is truly a non-reader, he will at least read the first chapter and then put it down. If he cannot put the book down, the teacher would know that he has succeeded in reaching this student. To the teacher's consternation, the student did not read one chapter from either book!

The teacher's last resort is more drastic. He recommends that the student's parents enroll him in a *speed-reading course* at a local college. With some hesitation, the student took the course and performed so well in the course that he actually began reading books!

The speed-reading course simply attached a stimulating, physical act (kin-esthetic/eye movement) to reading. Initially, the student was reading only 100 words a minute. After taking the speed-reading course the student was reading 300 words per minute! Now he could read a book in half the time; his reading comprehension also improved and school no longer remained a chore.

Parents and teachers are constantly faced with non-readers, and the key is to look for several solutions—even extreme choices such as speed-reading instruction. Speed-reading allows the reader to move rapidly through the essence of the material, discarding the extraneous language. Comprehension is also improved due to the fact that the kinesthetic learner's brain is now active with speed-reading and consequently more able to absorb information.

Lastly, for the purists, speed-reading might appear as a heresy to the writ-ten word, but the fact that a non-reader can sit down and actually read a book is the reward. Bottom line—if it works for some students, then go with it—as in reading between the lines.

Chapter 17

Food for Thought and the Knowledge
We Teach Our Children

Never have the words *you are what you eat* been more important than with children and their ability to learn and express their true intelligence. You do not have to be a genius to link school success to good food habits.

The by-products of poor eating habits show up in child obesity, ADHD or ADD, and eating disorders to name but a few. Other by-products could be school failure or simply a negative effect on the child's learning potential and intelligence. We read only about good nutrition but something else is missing which is that families need to prioritize good food habits.

In other words, if school success is associated with good homework habits such as consistency, organization, and responsibility another antecedent to school success should be a family's eating habits, particularly when associated with your child's learning potential and intelligence.

Parents need to make meals the one time of the day when all family members sit down together. Of course one should expect challenges to such a schedule. The average family's day is filled with so many activities that it is next to impossible for all members to do a sit-down meal each night of the week.

However, parents should find at least one night a week when the family meets for dinner. I suggest Sunday night because it precedes the school week and provides a good time to go over the upcoming school, social and family activity schedule. Further, it could also be a time to give appreciations of family members, which helps in forming family unity.

To teach good eating habits, another strategy is for each person in the family to be responsible not only for helping to plan and prepare the meal, but if possible to accompany the parents to buy food. Again, meal planning can be done on Sunday nights when the family makes its food list for the week.

A final suggestion is about nutrition and education in our schools. Although schools do try to incorporate health and nutrition into their curriculum, I believe they need to take nutrition to a higher level. If teachers are required to teach from mandated curricula why not include nutrition?

Nutrition is the fuel that drives the brain for greater learning and intelligence. Schools could take an interdisciplinary approach by linking good nutrition habits to all subject areas beginning in kindergarten and concluding in high school.

For example, math students can compute caloric intake versus calories used during the school day, which can include graphs and so forth. Science lessons could include the various chemical components of the food students eat, and particularly what, how, and why certain foods are better for you than others. Nutritionists should be regular speakers at all class levels. Lastly, school can have a nutrition week or fair where all the classes participate in a national fact-finding contest, reporting on food topics, nutrition, and their relationship to good health.

You are what you eat should not be simply a cliché that adults throw around whenever convenient. In short, the food our children put into their bodies should be as nutritious as the knowledge we teach them.

Chapter 18

Stolen Childhoods

Recently, an alarming statistic described the onset of puberty as beginning to occur at an earlier age for American girls, with many girls as young as seven and eight. New research shows that 10.4 percent of white girls, 23.4 of Afro-American girls, and almost 15 percent of Hispanic girls (Pediatrics, 2010) have displayed signs of early onset puberty.

Early onset of puberty begs the question: who or what is stealing the childhood of this age group of girls? I researched the probable causes for the early onset of puberty rates among America's children and discovered studies that attribute early onset puberty to the hormones that are used in cattle feed. The study suggests that the hormones in beef could be causing an acceleration of puberty in American's children (*Journal of Public Health Nutrition*, 2010).

Further, the use of the so-called stealth estrogens is why the European Union has banned the import of most North American beef, which is hormone treated. The ban has been a major dispute under consideration at the World Trade Organization.

Another hidden but insidious cause of early onset of puberty is the presence of many environmental toxins, which act as hormone-disruptors. In his book, *Our Stolen Future* (1997), Dr. John Myers of the United Nations highlighted the toxic effects of some of the estimated 70,000 chemicals in commercial use. Dr. Myers believes that some shampoos, for example, contain almost the same amount of hormone, as do low-dose estrogen patches, which are used for hormone replacement therapy in postmenopausal women.

A study by the American Academy of Pediatrics (2012–2013) describes that the age of onset of puberty for girls is controlled by the value of *fat stores* in the body. Enough fat in the body signals to the brain that there would likely be enough food and nourishment available if reproduction were to happen. In other words, improved access to food and nutrition has caused this change, particularly over the past twenty years.

The availability of food is a catch-22. Girls may have access to more food, but that doesn't necessarily mean that the food is nutritious, or that the availability of food is leading to a secondary problem of obesity, which is also a cause of earlier puberty.

Furthermore, the problem of early onset of puberty affects children's social development as well. In other words, early onset of puberty for girls goes beyond the physical. They may look more mature but they still have the emotions of young children.

For boys, with the exception of stealth hormones used in beef and environmental toxins, the connections between fat storage in the body and early onset of puberty is reversed when compared to girls. That is, studies have shown that fat storage of obesity in boys actually delays the onset of puberty, which can affect boys in other ways, particularly with self-esteem and body image.

Is the magic of full childhood gone? Statistics do not lie. Early onset of puberty is not only stealing childhood but may be also leading to other repercussions in later years of development. Will there be other health issues that they must face? Is anyone listening?

Chapter 19

A Story Well Told! The Lost Art of the Personal Narrative

Every child needs storytelling in his life. The personal narrative is the best form of storytelling, a form of literature which seems to have gone the way of the traditional telephone. The ritual of the oral tradition, family stories, which can carry over to the personal narrative and storytelling, has been lost to the current student population.

In my time, storytelling was often connected to school and family. At the end of the school day our teacher would dim the classroom lights and read from her literature book. Heads would go down and we would rest on our arms. We would close our eyes and listen to her soft voice rise and fall, describing the dialogue or the features of the story characters taken from Brothers Grimm, Hans Brinker, etc. I can still recite several of those stories verbatim.

The same might be said of Sunday meals when our large Italian family would come together: grandparents, aunts and uncles, and cousins would all talk about the past and become storytellers recreating their own childhoods or personal narrative, however imperfect they were. Today's children are losing this valuable experience to electronics and media.

Recently, I watched an animated film that was shown to K-4 students at a school's family movie night. It was a wonderful evening as the children appeared in their PJs, holding their favorite pillows or stuffed animals as families huddled together on blankets.

The potential for the development of a personal narrative that children would someday tell to their own children about the family movies they attended with their parents at the school was in full array. What was missing, however, with the animated movie was that there was little or no story line or lasting dialogue for the children to hold. Potential dialogue had been taken over by the overstimulating graphics and sound that overwhelmed any storytelling and a potential personal narrative. Again, the power of electronics was taking over the children's brains.

We might say this all began with *Sesame Street* which was a great visual/ auditory aid to the development of reading skills, but it was based on the adult show, *Laugh In*. The creators of the show saw the need to stimulate the child's working memory with short ten- to fifteen-second bursts of information.

Mr. Rogers was the ultimate storyteller and gave children the opportunity for the personal narrative as he slowly and softly described his daily personal narrative to his young audience. The end result of the long narrative was not only expanding the child's working memory (focusing and processing skills) but was also stimulating the limbic system and the hippocampus which is the part of the brain that forms positive relationships with the learning process.

The beauty of the personal narrative or story is that it can promote emotional and psychological stability and keep our brains regulated. The personal narrative can ground our experience in a linear way and even promote greater problem solving that can serve as blue prints for a positive emotional identity with our experience and environment.

The combination of a linear storyline and visual imagery woven together with verbal and non verbal expression of motion activates the left (verbal) and right (visual) sides of our brains. Include the frontal lobes (organization), the hippocampus (relationships), and even the amygdala (lowering the fight or flight mechanism) and the personal story or narrative can become an everlasting aid to healthy child and/or brain development.

Further, teachers are aware of the importance of linking storytelling to reading. Perceptive parents often read to their children at bedtime re-creating lasting personal narratives. Rudolf Steiner (Waldorf education) recognized the need to link the child's storytelling brain to the personal narrative when he long ago developed curriculums based on mythology (Norse mythology).

Clinical psychologist Louis Cozolino sums the personal narrative and/or storytelling best: "*A story well told, contains conflicts and resolution, gestures and expressions and though flavored, connects people and integrates the neural networks.*"

Chapter 20

I Learned It by Heart!

Joseph Chilton Pearce, author of *Magical Child* and many books about how to stimulate children's intelligence and learning, believes that the heart plays an important role in learning and intelligence.

According to Pearce, a nerve runs directly from the heart to the mid brain, the area of the brain where thinking is linked to emotion. For example, think back to a time when you became so enamored by a particular school lesson or activity that you lost track of time. Remember how smart you felt.

Pearce believes when the heart is stimulated in a learning situation, the midbrain is stimulated as well, and with the help of the chemical melanin, situated both in the heart and midbrain, you get greater learning and intelligence. Hence the statement *I learned it by heart!*

Notice your child when they are most focused, and it is almost always a situation when their learning involves something they passionately love to do. In my opinion, Pearce's theory supports Harvard psychologist, Howard Gardner's theory of multiple intelligence. That is, discover what the child feels smart about and greater learning and intelligence often ensues.

Richard Felder of North Carolina State University has expressed similar beliefs about learning and intelligence. Felder defines eight learning styles (active, reflective, visual, spatial, verbal, global, intuitive, and sequential) that are somewhat similar to Gardner's eight intelligences, as well as supportive of Pearce's belief about learning and intelligence.

Two of Felder's eight learning styles are called the *active* and *reflective* learning styles. We have all witnessed the active learner: they are children who cannot sit still at a desk before they are literally hanging over its side or simply standing at their desks when learning (Nobel Prize Laureate Earnest Hemingway might have been described as an active learner because he wrote his novels standing up at his fireplace mantle).

Furthermore, active learners are often the first students to raise their hands in class discussions and often the first to finish their tests! On the other hand, reflective learners must digest every bit of information slowly before they will ever raise their hands to comment on a question and often the last to finish their tests.

Sadly, during many classroom discussions, reflective learners often are left out because active learners always seem to get their answers out first and beat them to the punch! However, give the reflective learner time, and they will usually give a very well thought-out statement and even a brilliant answer.

Obviously, we should not simply label a child as active or reflective since children often match their learning style or intelligence to the lesson at hand. However, we still need to respect various learning styles: the active learners' bodily needs to move about when learning or to allow the reflective learner more time to process information.

Regardless of what learning style your child displays, active, reflective, visual, etc., the responsive parent or teacher should take the time to discover their child's learning style as another strategy to stimulate greater learning and intelligence. Observing your child in a passionate learning situation is one way. The other is to explore the many books associated with our authors, and remember Pearce's belief that great learning and intelligence must go through the heart first as in *I learned it by heart*.

Chapter 21

The Fantasy Advantage

Recent research by Dr. Deena Weisberg called *The Fantasy Advantage* describes new findings that suggest children absorb some lessons better when they are wrapped in magic and imagination.

For example, one of the strongest points about the Montessori philosophy is to allow children to use their fantasy with play. In other words, Montessori teachers are expected to stand on the periphery when a child is engaged in educational play and only intervene when the child asks for help. Further, one only has to walk into a Waldorf classroom to truly appreciate the use of fantasy and imagination that are incorporated into their curriculum.

Studies conducted by Dr. Deena Weisberg show that some lessons are better when they are wrapped in magic and imagination. She writes, *"In the past, psychologists believed that imagination activities were frivolous and actually prevented children to develop into mature thinkers."* She adds, *"What is emerging is that play is a crucial component for children's development. Further, advocates call for free play and that unstructured time for imagination activities can help kids be happier and more creative and sociable."*

A study conducted in 2005 (Bratton, S. C.) investigated hospitalized children who engaged in therapeutic play such as role-playing of medical scenarios and props showed fewer hospital-related fears than those who engaged in other types of play.

Weisberg and her colleagues proposed a *misplace theory*. It describes why aspects of the environment can set the stage for particular kinds of thoughts and behavior. She says, *"When the environment is realistic, children know not to expect anything out of the ordinary and can proceed as usual. But fantasy scenarios signal that kids need to pay attention because things in the environment do not necessarily follow the typical script."*

In another study, Weisberg and her colleagues enrolled 154 children from low-income preschools in a two-week education program. She read to half of them *realistic books* on themes such as cooking and farming and the other half fantasy stories with elements such as dragons and castles. In the course of reading, they taught the children new vocabulary. After each reading session, she gave the students the opportunity to engage in pretend play with stories that represented characters or objects in the books.

Overall, the program was a success. Both groups learned the new words that were taught. But the kids who heard the fantastical series were better able to tell researchers about the meaning of the new words than those who had heard realistic talks, showing important growth in their productive vocabulary.

And for adolescents and older adults, she concluded: *"It may be too soon to speculate how fantasy's educational power plays out with older children and adults, but it is certainly likely the same advantage would remain in some degree."*

Chapter 22

Our Job as Teachers and Parents

Certain industries use deception to attract children to buy their products. For example, why has the tobacco industry never had a problem with candy cigarette companies replicating their cigarette packs or why has the gun industry allowed close replicas of assault rifles as copycat-like toys?

McDonald's discovered long ago that if an industry gives toys to children under the guise of a side benefit of eating fast food it could create lifetime consumers. In other words, fast-food manufacturers realized that if you attach something fun and magical to a product you could make the experience a long lasting memory. One study showed that Ronald McDonald is the second most recognizable character in the world, second only to Santa Claus!

Interestingly, the toy gun industry seems to have had a free rein in the replication of guns for our children. Last year, in a second attempt to introduce toy-gun legislation, a state senator from D-Los Angeles sponsored a bill that would have required any pellet gun sold in California to be manufactured with transparent or brightly colored bodies to eliminate any deadly confusion. That bill died in committee.

This brings me to the issue of toy guns and the tragic death of a thirteen-year-old boy who happened to have a toy AK-47 gun replica at his disposal. We do not need to ask why a thirteen-year-old would want an AK-47 replica that shoots pellets. I desperately lobbied my parents for the BB gun, but with no success. Children see adults using guns in violent acts on TV, movies, and video games all the time. The power a child feels with a toy gun that actually shoots objects gives the child a false sense of power. Or, protection? Excitement? Identity?

The child's brain develops rapidly, when the frontal lobe, our highest center of the brain associated with higher order thinking, reaches maturity (early twenties). However, it is before fourteen when the essential molding of character takes place. Those early years are the time period during which parents need to realize the negative impact of various industries.

For example, from ages two to six, called the magical period, what a child sees on film, TV appears as reality to the child. The magical period is further reinforced when the child's brain secretes feel good chemicals (serotonin), which then attaches positive emotions to the learning experience.

It is during this age, between two and six that the child is most vulnerable to the power and manipulation of certain seductive industries that cater to children. Therefore, when children observe a violent act, be it with gun or any other weapon, the experience seems real, particularly when their guy wins. Again, such heroes of whatever magical industry are equated with power and importance.

Further, when children pretend to smoke (candy cigarettes), it is not only the power of the image of smoking, but also the candy (sugar) that can stimulate the lasting memory as pleasurable. Moreover, this magical stage is also highly kinesthetic or physical. That is, the power or positive feelings of play become attached to movement, be it with pretend smoking or play shooting.

Between ages seven and eleven cognition (thinking) and emotion (feeling) become more sophisticated. This age group sees the world in black and white. Fairness dominates their psyche. If some kid down the street has an AK-47 that shoots real objects, then it would be fair for them to have one as well.

The point of this article is to expose what we all know about certain industries that attempt to mold children, to create lifelong consumers of their product, at an early age of development. The goal of these industries is pure profit, especially when they can tap into a market that produces a percentage of children who could eventually become consumers.

Lastly, these industries will fight and lobby to the extreme for their products to be accepted, regardless of the impact on the well-being of children or society in general. Therefore, parents cannot rely only on government regulators to protect their children from these industries. They need to think out of the box and like my fifth grade teacher, expose their children to the truth of the seductive motives behind industries whose only goal is merely financial profit.

Chapter 23

The Value of Money and Social Consciousness

Just as parents need to expose children to vocational intelligence, the same need for exposure should apply to social consciousness and the value of money. For example, early childhood ages two to six is a magical time, and most children's perception of money is often associated with play or fantasy. However, parents need to be sensitive to this period and not rob children of this *magical connection* by beginning an allowance too early.

Most experts recommend ages five or six as a time when parents can begin to make children aware of the value of money by attaching an allowance to simple household chores such as setting the table, feeding pets, etc. The amount of the allowance can vary but usually it should be $1 for every year of age.

At this stage most children can only entertain one idea at a time, so parents need to keep the value of money, allowance, and chores simple. Ask this child how much money he or she thinks mommy or daddy earns and the image could range from $10 to a *zillion dollars!* Therefore, their perception of the value of money is often based solely on what they understand or perceive, which is often slightly right or left of reality.

One strategy is to attach household chores and allowance with a toy bank. When the child has saved up enough money, he or she can have a special visit to a toy store for a special gift or even a gift for a family member. When parents place a face on the value of money, they not only begin to raise the child's social consciousness but intelligence as well.

With the seven- to eleven-year-old age group, parents are dealing with a stage of development during which time children become collectors, consumers, and entrepreneurs. Therefore, be prepared to spend time bartering on why their allowance should be raised. They can entertain two perspectives at a time of fair versus unfair. If an older sibling's allowance is $15 a week the seven- to eleven-year-old will expect the same because it is only fair.

A friend's ten-year-old suddenly decided that it would be fair to be paid for every household activity he performed: 10 cents for turning on or shutting off a light, 15 cents for taking a dish to the table, and so forth! Fortunately, at this age parents can begin to stimulate children's social consciousness or the ability to move beyond fair versus unfair and expand their perception of the value of money by having them serve as a volunteer. For instance, the humane society is an excellent example for raising social consciousness because it places a face on the child's potential donation and the value of money.

The eleven- to sixteen-year-old begins one of our most sophisticated stages of cognition, having now achieved the ability to entertain more than three operations at a time. At this stage the value of money and social responsibility takes on an entirely new meaning. Taking classes as a baby sitter and then working as a sitter raises the bar of social consciousness and value of money to greater heights.

In addition, with this stage come major expenses: cell phones, iPods; so, it is critical that their perception of the value of money be also connected to budgeting. Just as the seven-to eleven-year-old can set up a saving/checking account, this age group should start thinking about setting up an educational fund, be it college or technical school. Again, such approaches induce long-range thinking and according to brain scientists stimulate the higher centers of the brain.

Exposing children to the value of money should not be looked at as an experience directed by the whim of the child. Rather, when developmentally appropriate, it can also produce higher levels of social consciousness and even higher levels of learning and intelligence. (Please see Lickona, T. "How to Raise Kind kids." Penguin Books, 2018).

Chapter 24

A Canine Solution to Reading Fluency

The past year a canine (pug) named Henry had the opportunity to spend a part of his day in a middle school English (reading) class. Anyone familiar with pugs knows their lineage or DNA is attached to the Chinese palaces of years gone by. In other words, a pug's entire life could be spent lounging on the lap of nobility or rulers while guests and visiting dignities conducted protocol activities associated with palace life.

The genus of pugs or any lap dog has the ability to sit and be attached to a human being's lap for lengthy periods of time—hence they refer to pugs as *velcro* dogs. In short, the longer the opportunity to sit on a human's lap, the greater their DNA is reinforced. The same held true with Henry and this class of middle school students.

Anyone who has ever had the opportunity to work with middle school students understands the dilemma one faces. That is, middle school students' brains are simply not fully wired. In other words, the brain doesn't reach full capacity to about age fourteen, which is why teaching middle school students is little like driving backwards down a freeway—you never know what is coming next.

The purpose of bringing Henry into the classroom was not only to ground/calm the middle school students but to be read to by those students incapable of sitting for longer than five seconds of reading time! Such students might be labeled as hard to teach or ADHD but for now let's just say these children have a difficult time sitting for any lengthy period of reading time.

A reading area was set up in the back of the classroom with couches and pillows to foster greater reading times for such students, but that was only marginally successful. Then the teacher enlisted the help of Henry, and low functioning readers were given the fortunate opportunity to read to Henry for thirty-minute blocks.

To the teacher's surprise the hard to focus students were able to read to Henry not only for thirty minutes but complained that they wanted more reading time! The Henry reading experience is supported by a study by Tufts Medical School (2011). The Tuft's study states: there are many health and psychological benefits of contact with animals, particularly for children. The study found that the presence of a friendly dog reduced blood pressure in children who were asked to read aloud to canines.

These benefits of the human-animal interaction could be used to make the learning process more comfortable and enjoyable for children. Furthermore, other dog assistance-reading program for students of all ages confirmed the same reading results in other schools when students were allowed to read to canines.

Therefore, what goes on in these hard to focus students' brains to foster such positive reading growth? That is, without a canine reading was marginally low with such children. One explanation is how the brain deals with incoming (reading) information. For example, information comes into the brain's thalamus, which is located in the lower centers of the brain. If the act of reading proves threatening or undesirable, then information is sent to the amygdala or fight or flight and reading or sitting for lengthy periods of time is compromised.

However, if the incoming information is nonthreatening, information is sent to the hippocampus where short-term memory is converted to long-term memory (cerebral cortex) for greater memory consolidation. In short, learning increases, or in our example, the length of time to read or for students to sit improves dramatically.

My recommendation to any teacher or parent with a student or child who has difficulties reading for any length of time is to employ a canine companion in your classroom to stimulate greater reading time. A dog assistance program is waiting for your call.

Chapter 25

Why French Kids Don't Have ADHD!

An excellent article written by Dr. Marilyn Wedge called "Why French Kids Don't Have ADHD" lists some major differences about the diagnosis and treatment of ADHD children in France versus the United States.

For example, the incidence of ADHD of US children has risen over the past twenty years from 3 to 5 percent to 11 percent (Wedge, 2012). However, in France, the percentage of children diagnosed for ADHD is less than 0.5 percent. Why the difference?

One major difference is that the French do not view ADHD as a biological-neurological disorder. She explains, *"The US MDs view ADHD as a disorder with biological causes and the popular treatment by US MDs is biological and treated with psycho-stimulants such as Ritalin, Adderall etc."* (Wedge, *Psychology Today*, 2012).

Dr. Wedge goes on to say: *"In France, MDs do not view ADHD as a medical condition but rather as a psycho-social and/or situational cause and as a result they rarely recommend stimulant medication."* In other words, French psychiatrists do not treat someone as psychologically abnormal when the behavior is often normal.

Also, French psychiatrists do not use the same classification system of childhood emotional problems as American psychiatrists or what is called the *DSM* (*Diagnostic and Statistical Manual of Mental Disorders*). Interestingly, the French Federation of Psychiatry developed an alternative classification system as a resistance to the influence of the *DSM*. France's version of the *DSM* or the *CFTMEA* (Classification Française des Troubles Mentaux de l'Enfant et de l'Adolescent—French Classification of Child and Adolescent Mental Disorders). The *CFTMEA* identifies and addresses the underlying psychosocial causes of children's symptoms and not on finding the best pharmacological band-aids with which to mask symptoms (Wedge, 2012).

Another significant difference associated with the French holistic psycho-social model has to do with nutrition. The French system connects ADHD-type symptoms or behavior caused by eating food, for example, with artificial colors, certain preservatives, and/or allergens.

Furthermore, in the United States, the focus is on pharmaceutical treatment of ADHD and often encourages clinicians to ignore the information of dietary factors on the child's behavior (Wedge, 2012).

In addition, from the time their children are born, French parents provide them with a *structure*. That is, children are not allowed to snack whenever they want. Mealtimes are at four specific times of the day. French children learn to wait patiently for meals, rather than eating snack foods whenever they feel like it (Druckerman, 2012).

The purpose of this article is not to accuse US parents of negative parenting, but rather to identify those with the knowledge and power who are not providing parents of ADHD children with a more intelligent and professional direction.

Chapter 26

Summer Slumps

Your children's summer vacation time can be one of the most pleasant and happy periods, but can also be a two-edged sword, if they fall behind academically.

For me, summer was filled with long days of swimming, playing ball, etc. However, there was one stipulation. As children we had to spend a period of the day reading or attending to some means of cognitive stimulation.

One of the most critical times of your child's learning brain occurs between early childhood and adolescence. This critical period also coincides with the primary grades to middle school, when academic proficiency is critical to their learning brain development.

Taking a two-month hiatus for even your most proficient students can cause a summer slump in academic skills. For the low achieving and at-risk student it could be catastrophic!

Brain development and academic skill development are not only based on maturity but also repetition and consistency. For example, you will almost always have a percentage of students whose academic skills are below the expected grade level curriculum; another larger percentage at or near grade level in the middle and another smaller group above grade level.

In 1996, thirty-nine studies found summer loss equaled about one month of classroom learning, and students tended to regress even more in math skills compared to reading skills. Interestingly, it also found that students from middle and upper class families improved in reading over the summer, while students from lower-income families regressed (Review of Educational Research, 1996).

Moreover, a Harvard University study reviewed research on summer reading interventions conducted in the United States and Canada from 1998 to 2011. The study included forty-one classroom and home-based summer reading interventions involving children from kindergarten to grade eight. Children who participated in classroom interventions, involving teacher-directed literacy lessons, or home interventions, involving child-initiated book reading activities, enjoyed significant improvement on multiple reading outcomes (Kim & Quinn, 2013).

The treatment group (those that received reading interventions), compared to the control group results (no reading interventions), was positive and included a majority of low-income children. Also, within-study comparisons indicated that summer reading interventions had significantly larger benefits for children from low-income backgrounds than for children from a mix of income backgrounds. These research findings identify the reading comprehension ability of low-income children (Kim & Quinn, 2013).

The significance of the studies shows that if families and educators encourage kids to stay engaged in learning throughout the summer, students may not only maintain, but improve their academic skills. Some advocates recommend year round schools and even summer school.

Unfortunately year round schools are not for everyone. For some families, the summer time can be a bonding time, for travel and summer activities, and summer school might be too punitive because many students who attend summer school are often those who are behind academically. Instead, the answer might be a cram course for parents to become more knowledgeable about how to remediate and/or teach reading.

Chapter 27

BPA: Why Parents Need to Be Concerned!

Why should parents be concerned regarding California's move to delay labeling of products containing a chemical commonly known as BPA or bisphenol? Please read below.

Today's children face dangerous environmental hazards that can affect critical developmental milestones, particularly brain development. According to a Northwestern Medical study (2011), the number of American children leaving doctors' offices with ADHD diagnosis has risen 66 percent in ten years. Moreover, in 1970, the rate of autistic spectrum disorder was 1 in 1000; in 2012, it was 1 in 88! Chemical scientists are identifying BPA as a potential environmental hazard for childhood developmental disorders.

BPA can be ingested into our bodies through consumption of animal fat. For instance, harvested fish from contaminated sites are the main source of human BPA contamination. Researchers have also found that shellfish accumulate BPAs as they filter feed plankton, and cows grazing on contaminated grasses and feed can transfer them into their fat, meat, and milk (Fitzpatrick, 2006).

Another potential hazard from BPA is that it is found in baby and water bottles, sports equipment, and used for industrial purposes such as lining water pipes. Studies show that BPA is released when one heats plastic bottles or plastic food containers (HHS, 2008). Epoxy resins containing BPA are used as coatings on the inside of many food and beverage cans. Since 2008, several government agencies have questioned how safe BPA is when used in plastic containers for the purpose of food storage.

BPA is an endocrine disruptor, which can mimic estrogen and has been shown to cause negative health effects in animal studies (Rubin, 2011). In fact, early childhood developmental stages appear to be the period of greatest sensitivity to its effect, and some studies have linked prenatal exposure to later physical and neurological difficulties. A 2011 study that investigated the number of chemicals to which pregnant women are exposed in the United States found BPA in 96 percent of women (*Environmental Health*, 2012).

In September 2010, Canada became the first country to declare BPA a toxic substance, and recently the United States has finally banned BPA use in baby bottles.

Overall, experimental evidence supporting the negative health effects of BPA varies significantly across studies. Some studies have shown that BPA presents no health risks to the general population; however, others believe that BPA can cause numerous adverse effects. The European Commission's Scientific Committee on Food along with the US food and Drug Administration believes that current levels of BPA present *no* risk to the general population. However, experts in the field of endocrine disruptors have stated that an entire population may suffer adverse health effects from current BPA levels (Endocrine Society, 2009).

If hormone disruptors have shown to effect early onset of puberty in girls, what effect do other chemicals which disrupt our endocrine system and mimic hormones in our bodies have on early brain development? Regardless of what school of thought is presented, it seems that the consumer will be the final decider, particularly when children are at risk.

Chapter 28

Intelligence and the Lost Art of Cursive Writing

Most children are taught to print during the first few years in grade school and, depending on the school, either they stay with printing throughout their school careers or they are also taught cursive, usually in second or third grade.

Is learning cursive still important in an age of texting and e-mail? Most definitely, yes! I particularly side with those who recommend teaching cursive handwriting as a strategy to stimulate brain synchronicity. That is, cursive handwriting helps coordinate the right side of the brain—or visual side—with the left side—or verbal side—of the brain. According to some researchers, the debate is a little like comparing the act of printing versus cursive to painting by numbers versus the flowing rhythmic brush strokes of a *true artist*.

For example, Rand Nelson of *Peterson Directed Handwriting* believes that when children are exposed to cursive handwriting, changes occur in their brains that allows them to overcome motor challenges. He says, *"The act of physically gripping a pen or pencil and practicing the swirls, curls and connections of cursive handwriting activates parts of the brain that lead to increased language fluency."*

Moreover, the work of Iris Hatfield, creator of the *New American Cursive Program*, also believes in the connection between cursive writing and brain development as a powerful tool in stimulating intelligence and language fluency. She says, *"The movement of writing cursive letters helps build pathways in the brain while improving mental effectiveness . . . and, this increased effectiveness may continue throughout the child's academic career."*

Further, Shadmehr and Holcomb of Johns Hopkins University published a study in *Science Magazine* (August 1997) describing how their subjects' brains actually changed in reaction to repetitive physical instruction. The

researchers provided PET (positron emission tomography) scans as evidence
of these changes in brain structure.

Shadmehr and Holcomb explain:

> *"computational studies suggest that acquisition of a motor skill involves learn-
> ing an internal model of the dynamics of the task, which enables the brain to
> predict and compensate for mechanical behavior. During the hours that follow
> completion of practice, representation of the internal model gradually changes,
> becoming less fragile with respect to behavioral interference. Here, functional
> imaging of the brain demonstrates that within 6 hours after completion of prac-
> tice, while performance remains unchanged, the brain engages new regions to
> perform the task; there is a shift from prefrontal regions of the cortex to the pre-
> motor, posterior parietal, and cerebellar cortex structures. This shift is specific
> to recall of an established motor skill and suggests that with the passage of time,
> there is a under* lie its *increased functional stability"*.

How this connects with cursive writing and/or language arts is that the
so-called *regions of the brain* that were most affected in the Johns Hopkins's study were the cortex to the premotor and cerebellar cortex structures.
Interestingly, these are the same areas of the brain that are often associated
with increased abilities in the language arts, particularly with the cerebellar
cortex and reading, etc. Perhaps this could be a reason why my cursive writing program stimulated increased linguistic abilities when I incorporated an
intensive cursive writing program with my learning disabled students.

In addition, cursive writing ability affords us the opportunity to naturally
train these fine motor skills by taking advantage of a child's inability to fully
control his fingers. This means cursive writing acts as a building block rather
than as a stressor, and provides a less strenuous learning experience.

Parents can be the final deciders as to whether or not to use cursive writing.

You have the research; you have the child. I encourage you to give it a
try. Go to any school supply store and purchase a wide lined paper pad,
appropriate pencils, a white board to copy the alphabet, etc. And then merely
support their writing those thank-you notes in cursive or sit down with them
and practice together. Buy them a journal and suggest they practice in a daily
diary. It could be quite a learning experience for them and a sharing experience for you as well.

Chapter 29

Look Before You Leap: Misdiagnosing ADD and ADHD Children!

The increase in children defined as ADD and ADHD has skyrocketed over the past twenty years. The US surgeon general on mental health (1999) states that 3 to 5 percent of school age children have ADHD or ADD. Some reasons for this increase are due to greater knowledge and education by parents and schools. However, other reasons could be the result of misdiagnosis, such as developmental levels (school readiness), poor diet (processed foods/sugar), electronic gadgets (TV, cell phones, computers, etc.), single parent homes (divorce and separation), all of which can affect a child's focusing and organizational abilities.

In addition, the increased percentages are cause for alarm, especially since the preferred medications for ADD and ADHD children are usually stimulants, which according to some experts, can become a gateway drug and lead to hard drugs.

This article's intention is not to throw the baby out with the bathwater, or advocate no medication. Instead, I wish to take a different approach in supporting children who exhibit ADHD/ADD characteristics, and address other factors that can affect a child's focusing and organizational abilities and common characteristics of ADD/ADHD. The factors represent some of the aforementioned reasons for ADHD/ADD behavior.

Another factor rarely mentioned might ask the question: does the school curriculum or learning environment match up to the child's learning style or intelligence? In other words, most school curriculums focus almost entirely on the linguistic, mathematical, and logical worlds and often neglect other learning modalities such as art and/or the kinesthetic or physical learning modalities. Teachers understand and deal with this dilemma on a daily basis and must adapt their teaching to the linguistic, math, and logical worlds, all supported by mandated curriculums, testing, and even shortened school years.

Further, teachers are keenly aware that some children who exhibit ADHD/ADD characteristics exhibit learning styles, or intelligence that do not complement the verbal, math, and logical worlds of the school's curriculum.

Dr. Howard Gardner's work in multiple intelligences would be an excellent place to begin to support these *other factors*. Gardner defined eight different multiple intelligence types that support differences in the child's learning potential and true intelligence. For instance, one of Gardner's eight intelligences is the kinesthetic learner, or children who need to use their bodies to learn and express their intelligence. Such children are generally the ones who can be geniuses on the playground or in sports, but sit them in a desk for lengthy periods of time, and we often see ADHD characteristics.

Hemingway stood up at his fireplace mantel to write his best sellers, and Longfellow wrote his epic poems standing at his desk. In short, a child dominant in kinesthetic intelligence often needs an alternative learning environment that is less formal, one that allows him to have periodic breaks, or simply have learning areas that address his body's needs when required to read, write, calculate math, etc. Some classrooms have reading areas or areas where children can go to learn, rather than sitting in a desk, or at a table, for lengthy periods of time.

We need to identify those children who are ADD or ADHD and provide them with the appropriate interventions and support. On the other hand, we need to be vigilant and look before we leap when identifying children with serious organic identifications as ADD or ADHD. First, we need to address the child's learning style or particular intelligence before turning to learning disability labels.

Chapter 30

When Boys Get More Classroom Attention than Girls

Researchers indicate that teachers (unintentionally) give more classroom attention and more self-esteem building encouragement to boys than to girls over the course of the school day. A 2004 study by Sadker and Sadker showed elementary and middle school boys received eight times more classroom attention than girls! When boys called out, teachers listened. But when girls called out, the female students were told to raise their hand if they want to speak. When boys did not volunteer responses, the teachers were more likely to encourage boys over the girls to give an answer or an opinion.

Absent from the study were the factors of the biological differences between the sexes, factors which could justify the 8 to 1 ratio of difference in attention given to boys over girls. Due to differences in visual organization on a biological level, a girl's vision is different from a boy's. The composition of the male eyes allows for *natural attunement to motion and direction.* That is, boys interpret the world as objects moving through space.

In a class discussion, boys gravitate to the teacher-like object. The more a teacher moves around the room, the higher the stimulation for a boy, possibly leading to more learning. For girls it is almost the opposite. The teacher's constant movement can be emotionally disconnecting to the teacher-girl relationship, causing a reduction in interaction.

In addition, girls are more focused when sitting. Boys need to move around. Further, during a classroom discussion, in order to get attention, boys typically stand up in their desk area and raise their hand enthusiastically. When that doesn't work, they switch hands and call out for attention. In short, the more a boy moves around, the more blood flows to his brain, which not only helps him focus and increases learning potential, but also draws the teacher's attention.

Furthermore, girls hear differently. When teachers speak in a high tone, girls often interpret this as yelling. Girls think people are angry and can shut down emotionally when voices are raised. Also, girls have a more finely attuned aural structure, which means they can hear higher frequencies than boys, so they are more attuned to sounds. Teachers need to be aware of their voice levels and tones.

Conversely, boys enjoy discussions that are more matter of fact, loud, and direct. Also, since girls hear better than boys, teachers often (intuitively) sit boys in the front of the classroom, which would allow for more attention getting and recognition for boys. On the other hand, girls work best when sitting in a circle facing each other and find it more comfortable to learn in a group setting. Instead, boys often excel in a traditional class structure with desks lined in rows, which could support their more competitive energies and attention getting behaviors.

Moreover, girls do not like to take risks and often underestimate their abilities. Girls respond to stress as a threat which drives blood to the gut rather to the brain, placing them in a fight or flight persona. However, for boys, it's the opposite. They love to take risks and almost always overestimate their abilities.

Lastly, another possible reason for the 8 to 1 statistic is that boys tend to ask for reasons to support an argument and need to focus on finding the answer right away; girls are more sensitive to the emotions of others, especially when discussions center around problem solving; so they actually may become more reticent in a class discussion and simply wait their turn.

Attaching biological learning differences between boys and girls could change the entire perception of how boys and girls learn, gradually influencing the 8 to 1 statistic. Whatever the reasons, teachers and parents should take note of the differences, creating greater learning opportunities for both genders.

Chapter 31

Why the Right Side of the Brain Sees More than It Hears!

There has always been a subtle conspiracy about how the left-brain world dominates those who might be right brain dominant. In other words, brain scientists have long known that we learn and express our intelligence based on which side of the brain is more dominant. For example brain scientists define those who have left-brain dominance as gifted in the verbal, linguistic, mathematical, and logical worlds. Those who exhibit right brain dominance are gifted in the artistic, musical, and spatial areas. Finally, the majority of us, move easily from the left to the right brain without too much difficulty. It is called synchronicity.

Parents often see these traits almost immediately with their children. One child is gifted artistically and begins to exhibit right-brain dominance as the gifted artist or another child with left-brain dominance exhibits his linguistic abilities as the precocious early talker or reader. Again, although we move back and forth between each hemisphere some of us clearly show dominance in one hemisphere or the other and that can be problematic for the right-brain crowd due to the fact that our culture operates from a framework of left-brain systematics.

It is apparent that the left-brain world dominates the professional landscape such as the business sector and also our schools, which are dominated by mathematical, linguistic, and other logical curriculums. From your child's school curriculum to the high school exit exam we see left-brain dominance with reading, math, and written language testing.

Conversely, you would never see these same students tested for artistic or musical ability. In addition, students are not identified for special education services for their inability to draw or play an instrument.

Dr. William Gaddes (1985), neurophysiologist and author explains, "*Because so many elementary school programs stress the teaching of verbal skills most teachers teach more to the left hemisphere than to the right. For the child who is bilateral (uses both sides of the brain) there is no problem. The child who suffers left hemisphere dysfunction is frequently treated unfairly by the school system. His skills in drawing, construction, map drawing, etc., are frequently ignored since problems in reading, writing and spelling are apparent.*"

Let's look at the child with right-brain dominance and what he might experience on his first day of school. Right off he might have problems sequencing the school day when his parents ask him to recount his first day, or when the teacher reads a story to the class and the same child when questioned about the story line goes blank. However, if you ask the same child to draw the story line in pictures you would receive vivid characters and scenes regardless that he has forgotten some of the key points about the story.

Moreover, school gets worse when he must learn how to read. Because his brain sees the world whole spatially, not in segments, he instinctively and unsuccessfully tries to sight-read. Unfortunately, his attempt to sight-read affects fluency and comprehension because he cannot remember words or sequence what he is reading.

Consequently, he is placed in the lowest reading group and when the teacher tries to teach him phonemically he struggles because his brain only wants to learn whole to part. If he continues to have reading problems he could be diagnosed as learning disabled and attend a special education class for reading, written language, and even math remediation.

The solution for our right-brain learner might be to attend an arts centered school that focuses on his strengths rather than reinforce his weaknesses, such as a Waldorf school. A school such as a Waldorf school or Montessori program combines the arts and academics or the kinesthetic or sensory motor skills with the academics.

Parents of right- or left-brain children need to take note and always try to attach the child's dominant strengths to their dominant weaknesses. Such theories as Howard Gardner's multiple intelligences helps define the child's strengths and weaknesses and also provides examples as to how to better stimulate learning and intelligence with children who exhibit strengths, whether possessing right- or left-brain dominance.

Section III

EARLY ADOLESCENCE

Figure 3.1
istock.com/kali9

AGES ELEVEN TO SIXTEEN

*There were people up there . . . out there? . . . who had a good time in life.
I was beginning to realize I wasn't one of them. I just didn't fit in. I didn't
fit in at my old school. I definitely didn't fit at my new one.*

—*About a Boy* (movie)

It would be a mistake to simply classify all individuals into one period or stage called adolescence, beginning at age thirteen and ending at nineteen? As a result, I decided to break up the adolescent stage into two stages, early adolescence, ages eleven to sixteen and late adolescence to early adulthood, ages seventeen and older.

For example, anyone who has ever walked onto a middle school or high school campus will notice that the student body represents all sizes, shapes, and emotional/or cognitive make-ups.

Early adolescence or ages eleven to sixteen have also been referred to as the *second renaissance*. As noted in early childhood, our *first renaissance*, ages two to six are also due to dramatic changes in the child's developing emotional brain and physical abilities.

For example, our brain develops from bottom-up or from the cerebellum at the base of the brain to the cerebral cortex at the top of the brain. From early childhood to early adolescence we see the child's thinking influenced by the emotional midbrain or limbic system. As noted in Section I, the *terrible twos* is the result of a brain driven by the cerebellum's need for movement. Similarly, the early adolescent's brain is attempting to breakout physically but also socially and/or emotionally. Both stages are dealing with significant changes and demands that mimic behavior that is often incompatible with parental controls.

As you read the articles associated with this stage, be acutely cognizant of the different developmental levels associated with all our stages and do not expect that one size fits all, especially with the early adolescent stage. Many children are moving in and out of different stages based on their perception of what is safe versus not safe or what the peer groups' values, while the family and school should serve as their safety nets.

Chapter 32

How the Arts Can Raise Student Achievement

Due to the current mandated curriculum, a major dilemma students face in today's schools is a greatly reduced art integrated academic curriculum. Budget cuts have also contributed to the reduction of integrated curriculum. Brain scientists have documented that when a teacher combines the arts with the academics, he or she not only stimulates greater learning potential and intelligence, but also supports the psychological development of confidence and self-esteem, both of which lead to deeper emotional commitment to learning (Gazzaniga, 1998).

In addition, a study by Fiske (1999), demonstrated that students in arts-based youth organizations achieved higher scores when compared to the standard school population on questions dealing with self-worth, personal satisfaction, and overall student achievement.

Also, well-designed and executed art programs weaved into the academic curriculum have proved to increase academic performance (Fiske, 1999). In addition, research on successful art integrated curriculums has demonstrated that access to and participation in the arts helps decrease negative behavior by at-risk youth (NSBA, 2009).

The study of art increases performance in expressive and cognitive abilities for the student. Artistic expression develops essential thinking tools: pattern recognition and development; mental representation of what is observed or imagined; symbolic, allegorical, and metaphorical representations; detailed observation of the world; and the ability to move from abstraction to complex expression (Rabkin & Redmond, 2004; Sousa, 2005).

A study of high school student achievement illustrated those students who were enrolled in art classes demonstrated higher math, verbal and/or, composite SAT scores than students who did not take art classes. The greatest improvement with SAT scores occurred with students who had taken four or more years of art classes (College Board, 2001).

Further, SAT scores increased consistently with the addition of more years of art classes. That is, the higher the number of years of art studies, the higher the SAT scores. The strongest relationship with SAT scores was found with students who took four or more years of art and music classes, scoring 102 points higher on their SAT than students who took one-half year or less of art and music classes (scores 1,075 vs. 973) respectively (College Board, 2010).

Another study identified students who took acting classes had the strongest correlation with verbal SAT scores. Also, acting classes and music history, theory, or appreciation had the strongest positive correlation with high math SAT scores. And all classifications of art classes were found to have a significant relationship with both verbal and math SAT scores. Finally, students with one year or more of art and music classes averaged 528 on the writing portion of the test—forty points higher than students with one-half year or less of arts/music classes (466) (College Board Profile of SAT and Achievement Test Takers for 2001).

With decreased school budgets, school administrators need to step back and reexamine the ultimate role of our schools and student learning. Instead of concentrating on mandated test scores and curriculum that disregard the role of art in academic achievement, we need to be more observant and connect to the revealing statistics of these studies of art-integrated curriculum. Just ask the students. Or, merely observe their performance, socially and academically.

Chapter 33

The Politics of Learning—Is Anyone Listening?

The effect the California state school budget is having on your children's learning brain has become tragic, to say the least. According to a study conducted by the University of California—Berkeley researchers, when the high school student-teacher ratio is less than nineteen students to one teacher, there is a dramatic increase in the percentage of productive learners/teachers. If the student-teacher ratio is greater than nineteen students to one teacher, the number of discouraged students begins to outnumber the number of learning students, consequently affecting teacher success.

In the educational setting, this implies that classes should have a student-teacher ratio smaller than nineteen students to one teacher in order to have the most *effective* learning and teaching attitudes in the classroom. (The average CA public school class size in kindergarten through third grade has risen to twenty-five students, compared to twenty just two years ago. Average class sizes in higher grades have grown from about twenty-eight students to thirty-one [*Huffington Post* 2011]).

Another example as to how the state school budget is affecting children's learning is the high-pressured curriculum squeezed into a reduced school year. Nearly 60 percent of California school districts have reduced the length of the school year, and 30 percent have shrunk their teaching days to 175 days. The number of days students in the United States attend school is low compared to other industrialized countries. For example, Japan (243 days), South Korea (220 days), Israel (216 days), and Luxembourg (216 days), to name a few, remain as the countries with the most extended school year.

Other learning problems caused by the drastically reduced state school budget are numerous mismatches between children's cognitive developmental levels with the required curriculum that could also affect students' learning potential. Perhaps there is not enough time for developmentally immature students to catch up to a mandated 175-day curriculum. Also, the school's curriculum is often being taught on a schedule similar to that of some runaway train schedule? Again, a good example of this curriculum mismatch is when fourth graders are asked to learn long division, which is a formal operational exercise requiring students to entertain three plus ideas at a time, including their math facts. And, this formal operational skill of long division is being taught within a reduced teaching year. Unfortunately, most fourth graders are still thinking concretely or can only entertain two ideas at one time, and are less likely to grow into the next stage under classroom performance pressure. Such negative experiences can remain with some students throughout their lives.

To add credence to my argument that such learning environments reduce student learning and intelligence, we only need to look at the physiology of the brain. For instance, the learning process begins when information is taken in through the senses.

The information is quickly delivered to two major areas of the brain— either, the *amygdala*, a part of the brain whose primary role is the formation and storage of memories associated with emotional events, or directed to the *hippocampus*, the part of the brain noted for memory consolidation and the transfer of short-term memory to long-term memory. However, it is the *thalamus* that determines where the information should be sent. If the incoming information is threatening, negative emotions are attached to the learning process and instantly sent to the amygdala, which prepares the body for a fight or flight response.

The end result becomes the short-circuiting of long-term memory, located in the cerebral cortex, drastically reducing use of brain potential. Apply this fight or flight interpretation to a student experiencing a stressful learning situation, be it large class size, shortened school year, developmental delays, and even mismatch of a preferred intelligence and the child's ability to tap into the brain's learning potential is compromised.

Teachers witness on a daily basis the fight or flight behavior of struggling students or observe the parent dealing with children struggling with a difficult homework assignment. Conversely, in a positive learning environment (reasonable teacher-student ratios, a longer school year, etc.) information can be sent to the thalamus, then to the hippocampus, seat of memory consolidation, and finally to the cerebral cortex for processing and long-term memory and/ or greater learning potential.

The less effective high school teacher-student ratio, shortened school year, rushed developmental levels, and even mismatches with intelligence are negatively affecting children's brains and learning processes. Politicians hold the keys and have the power to choose what type of learning situation we create for our children: fight or flight or greater learning and memory consolidation. Is anyone listening?

Chapter 34

Transitioning to Middle School

The transition from elementary school to middle school is considered a major milestone in every student's life. It is as though your student has just worked seven years at the same company and now must move to another company. Instead of one boss, he now has five or six bosses. Instead of working in one office for most of the day, he must move to other offices every hour, five or six times. To make matters worse, if he or she is late getting to any of his offices his punishment could be time spent in his office after work and usually in a different office with other tardy workers.

I think you get the point about how difficult the transition from elementary school to middle school can be. Therefore, parents need to be keenly aware of this period and that certain students may experience high levels of stress until he has successfully made the adjustment to middle school. For some students, this adjustment could take a few months. For others, it could be even more extensive. The longer the adjustment, the greater the distraction from your student's learning potential and developing intelligence.

Erik Erikson, the noted developmental psychologist, called the seven- to eleven-year-old psychosocial stage *industry versus inferiority*, (elementary school) and the eleven-year-old and older stage *identity versus role confusion* (middle school). For the middle school student *role confusion* can come from many different sources. For instance, the difference in the physical size of middle schoolers is particularly difficult. Being undersized can attract harassment from bigger students; being oversized, adults often assume greater maturity and expectation.

Developmental psychologists like to compare the middle school period to a child standing on two blocks of ice. On one block is the pull of childhood and on the other block is the pull of adulthood. The problem—the blocks are pulling him in two different directions. Therefore, the major goal for parents is to listen to the gripes of your middle school student with a sympathetic ear as he or she tries juggling this new identity with bouts of role confusion in their new school.

Another suggestion is for parents to maintain contact with their student's middle school teachers. If your student is being harassed, do not wait until conference week but be proactive immediately. A week of pain can affect your child's learning brain for the whole year.

A further adjustment that is often overlooked by middle school students is opening their lockers! If they only have a few minutes to get to a class located in some distant building and they can't open the locker, at this age, they would rather end up in class late, than without the needed material for class. Suggestion: have them practice their combination locks at home. In addition to a good locker and/or time management strategy is to color code their different notebooks and/or book covers so they can quickly grab the needed book, thus saving time in getting to class.

Moreover, don't buy backpacks that can store fifty pounds of materials! The bigger the pack, the more they will put in it. The smaller the pack, the better the organization.

Furthermore, be sure to purchase a large wall calendar to hang on your student's bedroom wall. A wall calendar is an excellent strategy to remind students about important homework assignments and activities, as well as thinking about the future.

Also, in elementary school your student was given grades with checks or check pluses for excellent. In middle school they grade with letters and in-between grades like A- and so forth.

Last but not least, there is no recess. He or she will most likely have a short fifteen-minute break and a forty-minute lunch period. Thus, be sure he has a good breakfast and a good snack to nourish him until lunchtime.

This article has only touched on a few adjustments your student will need to make in his transition to middle school. The rest is up to you to research additional articles concerning early adolescence.

Chapter 35

Absentee Fathers and Youth Violence

Park rangers discovered an interesting problem occurring at an African elephant reserve that might shed light on the effect absentee fathers have on youth violence. It all began after bull elephants were removed from the main herd and shipped to another park, leaving only the females, babies, and adolescents.

For some strange reason park rangers were discovering a great deal of destruction and violence in the park. Trees were torn up and animals were violently stomped to death for no apparent reason. Ultimately, the park rangers realized the violence coincided with the bull elephant's removal from the herd. After some scrutiny park rangers determined that rampaging adolescent elephants caused the violence. Soon after, the bulls were returned to the herd and all violence ceased.

We could draw comparisons between the above example and the effect absentee fathers might have on juvenile violence and even the high school dropout rate.

According to one study, when male youth do not have a father figure in their lives, they often join gangs to fill that emptiness and look to gang leaders to fill that *fatherless* void in their lives. There is a critical connection between a father's absence, juvenile delinquency, and anti social aggression in our youth. The study goes on to say that the likelihood that a juvenile male will engage in criminal activity doubles when he is raised without a dad. In fact, 72 percent of adolescents charged with murder grew up without their father (Characteristics of Adolescents Charged with Homicide, 1987).

Furthermore, other studies show that school systems with above-average rates of father absence have nearly double the rates of school violence compared to those with below-average rates of father absence. Children who do not live with both parents are also more likely to carry a gun, assault another student, and assault a teacher. To put it mildly, father absence could be the single strongest predictor that a child will grow up to be violent or fall victim to violence. (Father Absence and Child Well-Being, 2004)

Moreover, fatherless children are twice as likely to drop out of school (National Fatherless Imitative, 2002).

Instead of focusing on juvenile violence, perhaps we need to also examine why fathers become absent in the first place? For example, unemployment was a significant factor for divorce as researchers discovered male unemployment not only increases the chances that his wife will initiate divorce, but also that he will be the one who opts to leave. Today the US divorce rate stands at about 50 percent or one out of every two marriages ends in divorce.

In my opinion, although the problem of youth violence is the result of many factors, why not be preventative and enact a safety net to help fathers stay in their marriages and/or homes to avoid the absentee father dilemma and juvenile violence and the school dropout problem? In this day and age of high employment, cut backs in education (junior college), and apprentice training programs, etc., there should be no excuse or lack of money needed to address this problem.

Bottom line: it would seem to be a win-win solution. Investing in jobs could address the absentee fathers problem, lower juvenile crime, and the school dropout rate with one sweep. It makes sense.

Chapter 36

Contracts, Adolescence, and Family Values

There will come a time in every parent/adolescent relationship that a *behavioral contract* should be considered not only for your sanity but also as a way to stimulate the adolescent's problem-solving abilities and acceptance of family values. Parents need to take a proactive approach with behavior contracts. Why wait until the adolescent's behavior becomes a challenge to your family values?

For example, behavior contracts are developmental. Most adolescents possess the ability for higher order thinking or to think abstractly. However, this ability to support family values can be short lived. That is, adolescents often regress in their behavior because of conflicts between family values and the pull of the peer group. Such adolescent behavior is especially troublesome when the peer group challenges family values associated with personal freedom and responsibility. It is often easier and more popular for the adolescent to go with the peer groups' demands than family values because of the adolescent's vulnerability toward sexual experimentation, driving a car, drugs, alcohol, curfews—the list is endless.

Therefore, to successfully deal with the many pitfalls challenging the adolescent's needs and family values the parent and adolescent should create a behavior contract that is concrete yet abstract. The concrete is the actual spelling out of the privileges and consequences in the contract. The abstract or higher order thinking is the actual negotiation, acceptance, and signature and follows the behavior contract.

Let's review some of the major points about how to write a behavior contract with your adolescent.

First, be specific about the purpose of the behavior contract. Rules, privileges and rewards should be spelled out concretely. In other words, leave only so much room for them to stretch the boundaries because an inch can become a yard with some adolescents.

Second, be prepared to negotiate, since negotiation serves as a buy in for the adolescent and could foster higher order thinking. For instance, all parties should discuss the pluses, minuses, and interesting points of the behavior contract.

Third, the actual number of meetings and/or length of meeting time should be based solely on the contract's completion. I would suggest as many meetings as possible for completion and thirty to sixty minutes per meeting as tops out of respect for the adolescent's attention span.

Fourth, include only a few rules and behaviors. Too many rules and expected behaviors can set the adolescent up for failure.

Fifth, and worth repeating, adolescents are masters at stretching boundaries and distorting your words for their own liking, so keep the contract simple.

Sixth, again, be willing to reward positive behaviors. If a curfew is followed for one month, the contract can be revised, such as increasing the adolescent's curfew time by thirty minutes or the opposite for negative behaviors.

Seventh, *within reason*, the adolescent needs to feel they are equals in creating the contract. If they do not feel as an equal you could be negotiating the contact for days on end.

Eighth, be consistent and above all never put privileges and consequences into a contract that can't be obtained. This point is generally defined by your understanding of the limits of your adolescent.

My points represent the bare bones of creating a contract. You can add or subtract from my suggestions.

Lastly, remember, behavior contracts are *developmental*. The goal is to prepare the adolescent for the greatest behavior contract of all—which is their life and of course, respect for your family values and legacy.

Chapter 37

A Cause for High Recidivism Rates

One of the most difficult challenges for staff working in institutions for juvenile offenders is recidivism, or the return of a juvenile offender to "the hall" after a lengthy period of so-called rehabilitation. Staff are always elated by a low recidivism rate because it reflects the success of their work. However, seeing a juvenile offender return to the hall has always been painful, particularly when a staff member has spent so many hours trying to turn offenders into becoming successful law abiding citizens.

A young offender's return to the institution begs the questions—what could we have done differently and what is causing the repeat offences? For the moment, let's disregard their involvement with drugs, alcohol, gangs, etc. but instead focus on their failed moral reasoning (judgment of right/wrong). These offenders are very much like students in school who are failing and simply need academic remediation.

In this case, the remediation should be more related to moral reasoning, which is often left out of the intrinsic causes of their becoming juvenile offenders in the first place. A study by the Washington Department of Corrections showed that 73 percent of adult offenders had previously spent time in juvenile hall, an alarming statistic that reveals that our juvenile correctional system is often ineffective. Perhaps we need to truly investigate the causes of recidivism?

For example, in 1973, Dr. Lawrence Kohlberg and a team from Harvard University's Center for Moral Education successfully lowered the recidivism rate at a juvenile correctional institution by using hypothetical dilemmas to raise juvenile offenders' moral reasoning. Prior to conducting the groups the recidivism rate was about 33 percent. Two years later the recidivism rate was lowered to 18 percent. The lowered recidivism rate was achieved because the

Harvard team challenged inmates' moral reasoning with hypothetical moral dilemmas that were slightly higher than juvenile offenders' moral level.

A major moral dilemma that juveniles face is car theft. The reasons I have heard as to why juveniles steal cars is almost ridiculously simplistic, revealing a lack of judgment as to why juveniles break the law: *I know how to drive, but I don't have a license. . . . It's unfair that I'm not allowed to drive, so I stole a car.* Instead of focusing on the fact that they stole a car, why not focus on the why or the absence of moral reasoning that initially caused them to steal the car.

According to Kohlberg most juvenile offenders see the world in black and white, or they think only in twos such as fair versus unfair, which may define why they steal a car, which also demonstrates why their moral reasoning is so delayed. That is, when staff address the moral reasoning or the whys of juveniles' criminal behaviors, they now can access valid research as to how to remediate these behaviors.

A study conducted by the OJJDP (Office of Juvenile Justice and Delinquency Prevention—April, 2000) reinforces this premise and scientifically provides causes and solutions to recidivism. The OJJDP evaluated 200 programs serving juvenile offenders. Of the 200 programs only 4 programs: individual counseling, interpersonal skills training, teaching family homes and behavioral programs successfully reduced recidivism (positive—consistent results), while other programs—multiple services, restitution, probation/parole, behavioral programs, community residential multiple services ("positive effects, less consistent evidence")—were at best marginally successful.

When juvenile offenders' institutions begin to include the study of moral development theory in their programs, we might begin to see a parallel with the Harvard team's success with their use of hypothetical moral dilemmas to reduce recidivism. In my opinion, and this is purely a hypothetical appraisal, those successful programs (counseling, interpersonal skills, etc.) raised juvenile offenders' moral thinking by addressing personal dilemmas through counseling, interpersonal skills training, etc. which, as a consequence, then supported a respect for the needs of family and community.

The moral of the story: juvenile hall must become that other place or group where moral remediation can take place. Equally important, we should spend as much time understanding the whys of moral judgment theory as we spend defining juvenile offenders' offenses and punishments if we really expect to lower recidivism rates.

Chapter 38

Putting the Genie Back in the Bottle!

One of the greatest problems parents and teachers will face is Electronic Screen Syndrome (ESS), the collective effect electronics will likely have on your student's learning brain. Today's students, aged five to sixteen, spend an average of six-and-a-half hours a day in front of a screen, compared with around three hours per day in 1995, according to market research firm Wakefield, J. (2015). Teenaged boys spend the longest, with an average of eight hours! Eight-year-old girls spend the least, or three-and-a-half hours, according to the studies. Screen time is made up of time spent watching TV; playing video games; consoles; using a mobile phone, computer, or tablet.

The effects of ESS on the child's brain with respect to sleep, diet, family dynamics, behavior, and school performance have all been well established as having detrimental effects on their learning brain. Dr. Victoria Dunckley's excellent book, *Reset Your Child's Brain* (New World Library, 2015) explores these detrimental effects, as well as offers solutions to controlling your student's involvement and usage of electronics.

For instance, ESS causes a hyper arousal of your child's sensitive nervous system that can become a pattern, creating dysfunction in school, at home, or with social relationships (Dunckley, 2015). A lengthy list of symptoms often reflects chronic stress and/or sleep deprivation. It includes irritability, depression, changing moods, tantrums, lower frustration points, poor self-regulation, disorganized behavior, oppositional-defiant behaviors, poor sportsmanship, social immaturity, poor eye contact, insomnia, learning difficulties, short-term memory, tics, stuttering, etc. (Dunckley, 2015). Further ESS can exacerbate psychiatric, neurological, behavioral, and learning disorders and thus help to account for the higher incidence of ADHD. (Over the past ten years the incidence of childhood ADHD has increased 50 percent).

Moreover, research shows that certain populations are particularly affected by ESS. More vulnerable are boys, younger children, and children with pre-existing psychological conditions or developmental learning and/or behavior disorders. However, a problematic family history, youthful initial exposure to screen time, and high amounts of total lifetime exposure have also been linked as precursors to the above symptoms.

Dr. Dunckley recommends that negative symptoms can improve and/or resolve with what she describes as *electronic fasting*, that is, the strict removal of electronics for several weeks. She describes a three-week fast or longer, which can have a positive effect on the child's brain. For example, within days the child's initial negative reaction—tearfulness, anger, arguing, and so on—subsides. Also the child's mood, attitude, and compliance begin to improve. The child begins to sleep better, and may go to bed earlier.

Within weeks meltdowns become less frequent or less severe, or both. The child's attention improves, sometimes dramatically, and the child stays on task more easily.

Within months, grades may markedly improve. Meltdowns diminish further and may resolve completely, and mood stabilizes further. The child progresses more quickly when learning attention-sensitive subjects, such as math and reading.

The beauty of electronic fasting is that the brain is moved from that surge-and-deplete cycle to one of organization and self-regulation. Unfortunately, the genie is out of the bottle and to enact a cold turkey response or an electronic fast approach might seem impossible for many ESS addicted children.

However, one strategy that parents could employ would be a combination of electronic fasting and a brain-training program called neurofeedback. Neurofeedback has been defined as the Level 1—Best Support for Attention and Hyperactive Behaviors by the American Academy of Pediatrics (2013).

ESS is a highly addictive stimulus that affects our brain's ability for organization and self-regulation. Bottom line: neurofeedback helps the brain to self-regulate, become more organized, calm, and focused, the opposite effects of ESS. Applying both approaches could soften the extremes of electronic fasting and (maybe) put the genie back in the bottle.

Chapter 39

Your Students' Leisure Brain

One of the least discussed yet critical causes for student success is the ability for the student to experience what brain scientists call the "leisure brain." This condition of the brain occurs when a student's brain can breathe in a relaxed manner, taking in impressions with no pressure. With this environment, the brain allows for a processing that brings about greater organization and reassessment of the person's state of being.

This leisure brain condition is similar to the act of taking a deep breath before taking action. For some students the leisure brain is a natural act, but for others, particularly children diagnosed as ADHD, RAD, etc., the leisure brain is almost never experienced! Herein lies the problem. Without the opportunity to experience a leisure brain, such children are almost always in a state of high arousal or even of *fight or flight*.

This state of high arousal affects them socially, as well as academically. For one thing, adults only have so much patience and energy to deal with such a person on a continuous basis. Ultimately, the parent and/or teacher turns to an extreme solution such as medication as a means of taming the brain's unrelenting activity. Unfortunately, for some children the use of medication can become a downward spiral that can lead to addiction and eventually hard drugs. The short-term benefits: if you can boost the child's brain activity you can actually promote the ability to focus, which could resemble aspects of the actual leisure brain.

Students who experience a leisure brain regularly are the high performing students. High performing students have the ability to actually calm down the brain, which creates a greater ability for the brain to be organized (self-regulate), as well as focused. Another group of students experiencing this brain function are the athletic students who refer to the condition of the leisure brain as *getting in the zone*. Even while the athlete is confronting a challenge, the response feels effortless and unforced.

When an athlete or student finds the zone or leisure brain, he is, in reality, finding a pivotally functional spot that is indexed by the frequency of brain waves. The brain operates in cycles. For example, delta brain waves are 0 to 4 Hz, which is characterized by sleep or falling asleep; theta (4 to 8 Hz), a calm state that can be induced through meditation or disengagement; alpha (8 to 12 Hz) is our state of waking consciousness; beta 12 to 15 Hz, and high beta or 15 to 37 Hz, which often represents the brain waves of the ADHD child.

Finally, there is the *brain rhythm* referred to as gamma (around 40 Hz and higher), the brain waves of high performing athletes and/or high-powered business professionals. The key is to find that perfect zone in the alpha and theta range for what might be described as our "leisure brain."

Again, finding the leisure brain should be a given for parents of ADHD and RAD children. However, to induce the leisure brain through such practices such as meditation is particularly difficult for most children. Further, using medications will work only temporarily because the child's brain is in state of intense development, which can create unforeseen addictions or physical growth problems. One proven strategy which has the support of the American Academy of Pediatrics (2015) and has been especially successful with ADHD and RAD children is a brain training program called neurofeedback.

Chapter 40

School Success: Ability or Effort?

Is school success determined by ability? Effort? Or both? Psychologist Carol Dweck of Stanford University examined both areas and came up with some startling conclusions about school success. Dweck explains: *"because our society worships talent, and many people assume that possessing superior intelligence or ability—along with confidence in that ability—is a recipe for success."*

In fact, her research suggests almost the opposite. That is, when your entire focus is concentrated on intelligence or talent it can actually create the opposite effect, such as individuals who are vulnerable to failure, fearful of challenges, and unwilling to change. A survey conducted in the 1990s showed that 85 percent of parents believed that praising children's ability when they perform well got them to feel smart. However Dweck's research shows that praising kids' intelligence actually makes them feel fragile and defensive.

Further, Dweck believes that so-called smart kids can often coast through the early grades under the impression that no-effort academic achievement defines them as smart or gifted. Such children often believe that intelligence is a *fixed mindset* and to strive is simply not as important as being or looking smart. In addition, they see challenges as mistakes and even effort as threats to their ego rather than opportunities to improve.

Worse they can lose confidence and motivation when the work is no longer easy for them. Conversely, Dweck believes that teaching kids to have a *growth mindset* causes a focus on process (personal effort and effective strategies) rather than on intelligence or talent, which helps make them into higher achievers in school and in life.

Instead, she says, *"we should focus more on generic praise that suggests a stable trait"*—such as *"You did a good job drawing or I like the detail you added to the people's faces."* Or, *"I like the way you tried a lot of different strategies on that math problem until you finally got it."* Such praise for a specific process the child accomplishes fosters motivation and confidence by focusing children on actions that lead to success.

Dweck came to the conclusion that there are two views of intelligence or two classes of learners: the first are students who believe intelligence is a *fixed mindset.* This group views mistakes as blocks to their confidence that attacks their ability, which leads to the notion that if I have to work hard then I am dumb! On the other hand, the students with a *growth mindset* perceived intelligence as changeable that can be developed through education and hard work. In short, mistakes are actually challenging and energizing and offer opportunities for greater learning.

According to Dweck, *"such students with this mindset are destined for greater success and actually out-perform those students who viewed intelligence as fixed."* Moreover, she lists one study that compared two groups of sixth grade students who tested the same on a math achievement test. The following year the *fixed mindset* students scored one grade lower than the *growth mindset* students. Her research also looked at industry and in particular managers. She found that managers with a *fixed mindset* had difficulty taking suggestions and advice from others, whereas managers with a *growth mindset* saw themselves as works in progress and understood that they need feedback to improve.

The same might be applied to gifted athletes who are recognized as phenoms at an early age but flame out before they get to the big time relying entirely on their abilities rather than putting forth hard work. Bottom line? Students need to focus on process and hard work rather than purely on innate ability—the results could astound you!

Chapter 41

Electronics and Your Child's Novelty Seeking Brain!

A serious dilemma facing today's teachers and parents is the negative effect the gadgetry of electronics is having on our children's learning potential and/ or ability to focus in school. In short, this lack of focus might be directly attributed to our brains' need for novelty? In other words, our brain, as a novelty seeker, constantly scans environments for new stimulation.

Brain scientists discovered that novelty causes a number of brain systems to become activated, and foremost among these is the chemical, dopamine. The research shows that dopamine is more like the *gimme more neurotransmitter* (Poldrack, 2011).

It is very addictive, causing your student's consequent inability to focus in school. Of course, this addiction to the *dopamine hit* affects your child's learning potential and memory consolidation. Studies show that teens spend over seventeen hours a week on the Internet, fourteen hours a week watching TV, as well as countless hours on the cell phone.

The problem is even more pernicious when you begin to examine how the brain learns and retains information, especially when it comes to school and memory consolidation. Working memory occurs in many shapes and sizes. In the classroom, an adolescent's working memory lasts for about twenty minutes, the maximum prime time that most adolescent brains can assimilate information (Sousa, 2005). There will be a down time of about ten minutes and then another twenty minutes of prime time.

The problem with working memory and today's learner is that when the brain is conditioned by novelty seeking electronic devices, working memory and/or memory consolidation can be reduced and compromised. For information to be converted from working memory to long-term memory, there must be a period when significant emotional content (limbic system) and cognition (cerebral cortex) operate simultaneously.

For example, in a school learning situation, when the child's brain is asked to acquire information, the need for novelty seeking takes over and can shut down working memory in a way that limits his ability to transfer information to long-term storage. The statement that parents and teachers hear so often from students, *I'm bored,* could be the child's novelty seeking brain speaking.

Another problem created by our novelty seeking brain and electronics occurs with sleep. The adolescent's fixation with electronics often causes some students to interact with electronics into the early morning hours which short changes REM (rapid eye movements) sleep. Therefore, for effective school learning to be converted from working memory to long-term memory, the adolescent needs six REM (rapid eye movement) cycles per night (children and adults need one less hour). However, when students are deprived of sleep, they are not only limiting REM sleep and memory consolidation, but worse, making themselves vulnerable to a serious disorder called SDS (sleep deficit syndrome).

When the brain is conditioned to *novelty seeking attractions,* the end result can be children who never truly focus (intensely) on one or two particular interests, but instead, on several, in order to keep the novelty seeking brain satisfied. Also, when the brain is conditioned to novelty seeking attractions, there can also be a strong need for students to seek other forms of novelty seeking attractions such as drugs, which is why stimulants and poor diet (sugar/soda) can be so harmful to our children's ability to focus and learn.

Years ago, novelty seeking was more grounded. Life moved slowly. We spent our time reading books rather than attached to electronics or taking walks in nature instead of lying on the couch watching TV or surfing the Internet.

Our children's brains need time away from electronics. Daily meditation, reading, nature walks, knitting, etc. are essential to control the brain's powerful need for novelty seeking attractions. Am I missing anything?

Chapter 42

When Underachievers Affect School Test Scores

An underlying factor affecting the validity of mandated school test scores is the impact of the scores of underachieving students. Underachieving students present an entirely different problem for teachers and parents, presenting performance scores that do not often reflect a teacher's ability to teach or a parent's ability to parent. In short, the underachiever's behavior is so deeply engrained and difficult to change that unless corrected, his learning style can become a lifelong debilitating disorder.

Studies have defined *four* particular underachieving types that teachers and parents deal with on an everyday basis. For example, there is the *distant underachiever* who is afflicted with abandonment issues caused by adoption, multiple moves, death of a loved one, traumatic illnesses, divorce, etc. Their fear of abandonment is punctuated by a fear of failure, which undermines any and all forms of achievement.

The second underachieving type is called the *passive underachiever*. Such students are often so well liked that their teachers and parents will go to great extremes to rescue them from failure. The end result is that these students are perpetually stuck in a fear of losing the support of teachers and caregivers—so they underachieve in order to receive the nurturing energy of concern and coaching.

The third type, called the *independent underachiever*, is someone who distances himself from help by demanding that he can achieve on his own. However, the independent underachiever starts and stops, and makes up excuses for his failures. Unfortunately, in his need to be independent, he fails to develop the necessary skills or tools to be independent, which is why he constantly underachieves.

Lastly, there is the *defiant underachiever*, who avoids an extreme fear of failure by using defiance to blame others for his underachievement. This group often resorts to school truancy, as well as extreme behavior problems both in school and at home.

One simple but effective strategy for parents and teachers to help underachieving students deal with failure is to define the underachiever's multiple intelligences. Dr. Howard Gardner of Harvard University defined eight particular intelligences (naturalist, math/logical, kinesthetic, musical, spatial, intrapersonal, interpersonal, and linguistic) that can actually offer some help to parents and teachers of underachieving students (Please see MIDAS (Multiple Intelligence Developmental Assessment Scales) for additional information concerning multiple intelligence). This can be achieved by tapping into the students' brain centers associated with underachievement and the students' relationship to failure.

When you attach the underachiever's multiple intelligence to achievement you are actually stimulating the brain's primal achievement centers associated with learning and intelligence.

The underachieving student is in a constant *fight or flight* response due to his fear of failure. Further, this *fight or flight* response directs learning away from the brain's hippocampus, our emotional and relationship component associated with successful learning, and instead directs the energy to the brain's amygdala, justifying the underachiever's constant fear of failure. The result is not only decreased learning potential and intelligence but also a lifelong pattern of underachievement leading to school failure.

Another simple strategy to help underachievers is to create a *behavior contract*. Underachievers need predictability, organization, and consistency, particularly with rules and boundaries. Rules create boundaries that allow the distant learner to trust; the passive learner to not wiggle out of responsibility; the dependent learner to sense empowerment; the defiant to help set his own rules. Finally, a contract empowers the underachiever. A mutually acceptable contract not only stimulates the brain's hippocampus (trusting relationships), but also activates the prefrontal cortex, seat of organization and executive functioning.

Underachievement can be a lifelong debilitating disorder, and teachers and/or parents, as their students, should never underachieve in the option of seeking assistance and information.

Section IV

LATE ADOLESCENCE TO EARLY ADULTHOOD

Figure 4.1
istock.com/kali9

AGES SEVENTEEN TO EARLY TWENTIES

The acquisition of any knowledge is always of use to the intellect, because it may thus drive out useless things and retain the good. For nothing can be loved or hated unless it is first known.

—Leonardo da Vinci

As discussed in our previous section about early adolescence, our final stage, late adolescence and early adulthood, can also be described as equally difficult. That is, we often think that adolescence begins at age thirteen and ends at nineteen. However, research shows that the brain is beginning to move to higher order thinking or full formal operational thinking as early as age eleven. Therefore, we cannot conveniently divide the adolescent stage into one stage of thirteen to nineteen. Instead, we need to be flexible with this period and extend adolescence from age sixteen to early adulthood, or the early twenties or *late adolescence and early adulthood*.

The importance of this stage is that this age group can think about one idea, while still entertaining additional ideas. With school it will be evidenced in curriculums requiring higher order thinking such as with the mathematics, sciences, etc.

For careers, it could be seen in college or vocational training that requires thinking out of the box. And for relationships, it could be experienced as becoming less focused on only one's personal needs, but also being able to take into account another being's needs and/or emotions.

The age extension to the early twenties is due to a variety of negative influences that can block higher order thinking such as economics or one's standard of living. For instance, many so-called early adults continue to live at home due to economics. In addition, some young adults lack job skills, leaving them able to earn only a minimum wage. Others are in college accumulating large debt, which locks them into a lifestyle that can be incompatible with marriage, school, starting a family, and a job with a future.

One approach to unblock this age group's so-called learning brain is through vocational assessments. (For additional information please see the Holland's Self-Directed Search.)

When you are able to define a vocational interest, you are also creating a vocational identity with one's intelligence to support higher order thinking and learning. In short, great achievement is often associated with a deep passion with a specific vocation at an early age. In high school Bill Gates would spend hours on end at a university computer lab. At age seven, Spielberg asked his parents for a camera, so he could make family movies.

Article #45 titled Vocational Intelligence—Just Ask Bill Gates! is almost a personal plea to encourage parents to reinforce a child's passion with a particular interest. For younger kids you need to observe them in play or listen to their conversation that says: *I really had fun building a fort*. These could be the remarks of a potential architect. Remember it is never too late to assess, but it helps to start early.

Chapter 43

Do You Know How Many Books You Have in Your Home?

If you are a parent you might consider taking a count of the number of books you have in your home. This may seem trivial; however, a twenty-year study by Mariah Evans, University of Nevada, and Reno, associate professor of sociology and resource economics, discovered that the number of books in a home has shown to raise the educational level of children in the home. That is, the difference in educational level of the children between being raised in a bookless home *as compared to* a home with a 500-book level was significant, regardless of parents' educational level.

Whether the parents are barely literate (only three years of education) as compared to parents who have a university education (fifteen plus years) proved not to be a significant factor in the potential educational level of their children. Having a 500-book library, however, raised a child 3.2 years in education! Moreover, Evans found that children of lesser-educated and economically disadvantaged parents would benefit the most from having books in the home (*Science Daily*, 2010).

She poses the question, *"what kinds of investments should we be making to help these kids get ahead?"* The results of her study indicate that getting some books into such homes is an inexpensive method for helping these children succeed. Further she found that having as few as twenty books in the home had a significant impact on moving a child to a higher level of education. In other words, the more books you add, the greater the benefit, (Education World, 2016).

Moreover, in countries such as China, she found that having 500 or more books in the home increased children's educational level 6.6 years. In the United States, the effect was less, 2.4 years, less than the 3.2-year average advantage experienced across all twenty-seven countries. But,

Evans points out that *2.4 years is still a significant advantage in terms of educational attainment.*

Evans was struck by the positive effect having books in the home had on children's educational attainment beyond such factors as the educational level of the parents, the country's GDP, the father's occupation, or the political system of the country. In short, having books in the home is twice as important as the parents' education level, and more important than whether a child was reared in China or the United States. Interestingly, the difference in educational attainment for children born in the United States and children born in China was only two years, or less than two-thirds the effect that having 500 or more books in the home had on children.

Evans believes that having books in the home stimulates reading, particularly with very small children. For example, simply talking about the books as the parent reads can make a huge difference. (Please see The Read Aloud Program.) Furthermore, homes in which books are used to stimulate intelligent conversation, rather than argumentation, serve as an important contribution to children's so-called learning strategies (Education World, 2016).

Evans goes on to say: *"When children observe what their parents do, reading at home is very important in a role-modeling sense. Children gain skills and culture/content from the books in the home. These skills and content even help children perform better on standardized tests. Bookish homes help children enjoy school and see their teachers as valuable coaches. Success in performance in school, leads to a positive relationship with school and education, encouraging young students to continue in education even when the going gets tough. I admit that this question contains quite a load of hypotheses, but that's how we suspect the process works."*

Therefore, as concerned parents, we should consider the impact on our children as they live in a home with or without books and with or without adults who actually take them off of the bookcase and read them.

Chapter 44

Groundbreaking ADHD Research

Parents of ADHD children often approach each school year with a degree of trepidation and disillusionment. They question: *Is my child truly ADHD or is it a developmental disorder that he or she will grow out of?* Worse, *If he or she has ADHD, do I medicate now and not worry about the potential negative side effects?*

In 2011, the prevalence of attention deficit hyperactivity disorder in children ages four to seventeen years was 11 percent, with 6.4 million children diagnosed with ADHD and 4.2 million taking psycho stimulants (CDC, 2013). This is a dramatic increase from more than thirty years ago, when the rate of ADHD was estimated at between 3 percent and 5 percent. And the prevalence of ADHD increased by about 35 percent from 2003 to 2011 and is still rising. In fact, more than 20 percent of high school-aged boys have been diagnosed as having ADHD (*New York Times*, 2013).

Complicating parents' disillusionment about ADHD and medication are the drug companies' aggressive marketing which has extended the image of classic ADHD to include relatively normal behavior like carelessness and impatience, and has often overstated the pills' benefits which has also led to over diagnosis (*New York Times*, 2013).

The problem with stimulant medication is that it can cause any number of serious side effects with your child's brain. According to ISMP (2014) studies of a list of fifteen potential drugs causing serious side effects, the list includes the three most popular medications for ADHD: Concerta, Ritalin, and Strattera. The following side effects associated with the three drugs are: suicidal behaviors, retarded growth, and some manifestations of psychosis, aggression, cardiac arrest, and weight loss or affected growth.

However, a University of Cambridge study (BCNI, 2013) questions past research, which suggests that ADHD is the result of fundamental abnormalities in *dopamine transmission*. Instead, the study defines the main cause of ADHD may lie instead in *structural differences* in the brain's gray matter which is responsible for decision making, focusing, language development, etc. Patients with ADHD, who had significant loss of gray matter in the brain, as measured by MRI (magnetic resonance imaging) and PET (positron emission topography), showed significant impairments in attention performance compared with healthy individuals (University of Cambridge, 2013).

In a recent publication, Emily Deans (M.D.) writes that *iron* is a key component to the brain's gray matter and vital for normal brain development and human behavior.

In a 2004 article in *Nature* magazine, Dr. Helen Pilcher writes: *"Size may matter after all, when it comes to IQ. A brain imaging study suggests that human intellect is based on the volume of grey matter in certain brain regions, challenging alternative views about the basis of intelligence"* (Nature, 2004).

Also, iron is a key cofactor in the making of neurotransmitters in the brain that affect neuron signaling, including serotonin, norepinephrine, and especially dopamine (*Psychology Today*, 2015). Further, studies show that ADHD in children is associated with low levels of serum iron and ferritin, compared to control groups of children without ADHD who had normal levels of serum iron and ferritin. In short, iron supplementation has also been shown to improve symptoms of ADHD (Deans, *Psychology Today*, 2015).

Moreover, professor Trevor Robbins, coauthor of the Cambridge Study, believes that her findings question the previously accepted view that major abnormalities in dopamine function are the main cause of ADHD patients. She goes on to say, *"while the results show that Ritalin has a therapeutic effect to improve performance, it does not appear to be related to fundamental underlying impairments in the dopamine system in ADHD"* (Brain, 2016).

Researchers have determined that ADHD may not be the result of abnormalities in dopamine transmission but rather the result of structural differences in the brain's gray matter.

Further, popular ADHD medications such as Ritalin, Strattera, and Concerta have proved to be particularly dangerous to children's brains. Again, current research suggests that parents take a different approach and address the gray matter of the ADHD brain and the possible benefits of iron supplements and the effect it can have on ADHD.

Chapter 45

Vocational Intelligence—Just Ask Bill Gates!

Vocational intelligence is a preference or a particular interest toward a certain type of vocation that usually comes by way of a hobby or interest in the child's play. Bottom line—it is never too early to make children aware of their vocational intelligence.

This does not mean that parents should program children into specific vocations. The world is filled with adults who work in careers, chosen by their parents, and who end hating the decision for the rest of their lives! However, great learning and intelligence can be experienced when you allow children to focus on activities they love to do. Again, expose, but do not indoctrinate professions.

For example, one of the most valuable experiences for many children occurs when parents give talks in the child's classroom about their chosen profession. In addition, *the bring your child to work* days has become a great experience for most children involved. Moreover, when the child is exposed to various careers you are not only attaching a face to a career, but in my opinion, it stimulates abstract thinking or areas of the brain where great learning and intelligence can occur.

Perceptive parents need to take the lead at home as well. For example, the child who never seems to get enough of nature could be expressing his vocational intelligence as a naturalist. Parents should consider enrolling such children in nature camps. Again, such exposure gives a face to the experience an obvious leg up on a future career, as well as gets their brains to think abstractly.

A recent study asked practicing physicians why they became doctors. A staggering 80 percent said they had experienced a personal death or tragedy in their childhood that motivated them toward a medical profession.

The recent publication of Malcolm Gladwell's book, *The Outliers*, traces the lives of highly successful individuals (Mozart, Gates, etc.) and theorizes that most of these successful individuals invested at least 10,000 hours in their chosen profession before they reached the pinnacle of success.

You would not expect individuals to be so driven or lucky enough to start so young in their lives to invest 10,000 hours; but again, parents can take the lead and notice certain interests and strengths with their children to reinforce the child's vocational intelligence. It happens all the time with great athletes, writers, doctors; so why not your child? A simple trip to the library, concert, museum, university, and so forth are ways to stimulate greater learning and vocational intelligence with children.

For example, I have used the Holland's Self-Directed Search (SDS) extensively with middle and high school students as a way to define future vocational interests. Some of my greatest successes with at-risk youth were due to vocational assessments. For the first time in my students' problematic lives someone was actually connecting their potential skills or interests to future careers and saying, *you can be someone*!

Regardless of the child's age or circumstance, the wise parent could begin to observe her child and provide opportunities for children to connect their vocational intelligence dots. From my perspective, it is never too young to begin to feed into a child's vocational intelligence. If it can happen with Bill Gates, it just might happen with your child as well!

Chapter 46

And Remember, It's Only a Test!

With finals week approaching for most high school students, here are some suggestions about how students can improve their test-taking skills or strategies. Students need to realize that doing well on a test is not based solely on the student's ability to recall information, but also on his or her knowledge about test preparation.

For example, the obvious and one of the most important strategies is to review regularly course content from beginning to end. This is critical. The earlier you review, the less you forget. Studies about learning and memory show that you will remember most information at the beginning and end and forget the middle. Reviewing the material will keep beginnings, middles, and ends current. Also, ask your brain how it likes to remember, and it will probably say, *review and review and review*.

Another important strategy is to learn the material in chunks or what learning specialists call *chunking*. And always remember the brain responds best to organization, and *chunking* supports good organizational skills.

The next obvious point is to think about what your teacher considers most important. We all know teachers have certain interests; therefore, their particular interests could be on the test.

Know vocabulary, special terms, or formulas for the type of test you expect. You would not expect to prepare a meal without knowing the recipe's language, so learn the test's language.

Form questions about the test and see if you can answer them. The more you practice, the more you are duplicating the test situation, which could eliminate test anxiety and/or performance anxiety. Professional athletes do this all the time—it is called *visualization*. Further, it helps if you close your eyes and visualize the test questions and answers. Try and see yourself going through all the emotions of taking the test.

Study end-of-chapter questions. This will reinforce the theory of beginnings, middles, and ends. Also reread review summaries, notes, outlines, and previous assignments. Furthermore, compare your notes with a friend. The notes are often only another version of the test.

Recite specific facts to yourself. You can do this when walking, driving a car, or riding a bike. This strategy ties in with theories associated with multiple intelligence and learning styles. That is, active and kinesthetic learners study best when they can use their bodies to learn or express their intelligence.

Get a good night's sleep—it is critical for successful test taking. Some of us are morning, afternoon, or evening people. If you stay on a schedule, you can learn to regulate your biorhythms or cycles supporting your physiological, emotional, or intellectual well-being or prowess.

Last but not least—eat a good breakfast the morning of the test. Again, most adolescents eat at all times of the day or nothing at all, which is why most nutritionists believe adolescence is the unhealthiest period of our lives. In short, the brain is an engine that needs to run on protein. Find a diet that you like and stick with it. Good luck and remember *it's only a test!*

Chapter 47

Teen Athletes and Performance-Enhancing Drugs

The ongoing saga regarding professional athletes and PEDs, performance enhancing drugs, minimizes the real problem concerning the consequences for players and drug suppliers. For years those in power have looked in the other direction when dealing with performance-enhancing drugs. That is, higher athletic performance means money to the athletes, as well as to their teams. However, there is something far more insidious beyond the consequence of a suspension or lost money for perpetrators. Instead, the discussion should focus on the effect such athletes have on our most vulnerable and impressionable audience—namely our kids.

An estimated 4 to 12 percent of US high school boys and up to 3.3 percent of high school girls have used anabolic steroids. A study by Buckley found that 6.6 percent of male high school seniors had tried steroids, with 67 percent initiating use by sixteen years and 40 percent using multiple cycles. These findings were later confirmed in studies of Indiana high school football players, as well as from a 2003 Center for Disease Control report. Prevalent studies extend to middle school populations as well (Orthopedics, Oct. 2008).

For teens, the most common performance-enhancing drugs and supplements include creatine, a naturally occurring compound in the body that is also sold as an over-the-counter supplement. It is primarily used to enhance recovery after a workout and increases muscle mass and strength. Creatine is popular with athletes who participate in football, gymnastics, hockey, wrestling, etc. Side effects include weight gain, nausea, muscle cramps, and kidney damage.

Another popular drug is the anabolic steroid. Anabolic steroids are synthetic versions of the hormone testosterone, used to build muscle and increase strength. They are popular with football players and weightlifters. Use of anabolic steroids can cause heart and liver damage and halts bone growth.

Finally, there are the steroid precursors. Steroid precursors, such as andro-stenedione (*andro*) and dehydroepiandrosterone (DHEA), are substances that the body converts into anabolic steroids. They are used to increase muscle mass. Most steroid precursors are illegal without a prescription. DHEA, how-ever, is still available in over-the-counter preparations. Side effects of steroid precursors are similar to those for steroids (Mayo Clinic, 2009).

If your child is using performance-enhancing drugs the warning signs are: behavioral, emotional, or psychological changes—particularly increased aggressiveness ("*roid rage*" as in steroid rage); secondly, changes in body build, including muscle growth, rapid weight gain, and development of the upper body; thirdly, increased acne and facial bloating and needle marks in the buttocks or thighs; finally, enlarged breasts for boys or smaller breasts in girls.

Parents can do the following. For example, educate your athlete not only about the ethics of drug use and cheating in athletic competition, but also, the health risks as stated above. Also, it is against the law to use steroids. Most steroid precursors are illegal without a prescription. Moreover, parents must take a zero tolerance when it comes to their child using performance-enhancing drugs. If you take drugs, you quit the team.

Get involved with your child's team. Visit the practices and get to know their coaches, etc.

Moreover find positive role models to speak to the player about the effect drugs can have on the human body. Monitor your teen's purchases. Check the ingredients of any over-the-counter products your teen uses. Watch for performance-enhancing drug paraphernalia. Finally, get in touch with your health care provider for additional support. It could be a key to your child's mental and physical health.

Chapter 48

Fear of Failure? Only in Your Mind!

Some of the most difficult students to teach and to coach are those who have a *fear of failure*. Unfortunately, for many teachers and coaches such students often display deep scars of failure that can challenge even the most experienced and successful teacher or coach. In my opinion, those teachers or coaches who possess the ability to change an individual's perception of failure have achieved the ultimate challenge in the classroom or on the playing field.

One strategy to deal with fear of failure is to focus on the student's cognitive/emotional areas (limbic system) of the brain or how they learn best? For boys, it can be anything associated with their kinesthetic intelligence or movement. This would confirm why studies show that boys learn best when the teacher is physically active or animated during a teaching lesson.

Conversely, girls learn best when the teacher is more stationary. The reason for this might be due to the differences in girl/boy limbic system. In other words, a girl's hippocampus, located, in the limbic system, represents a part of the brain associated with emotional relationships, be it social or academic. In fact, a girl's hippocampus is larger than boys. On the other hand, the amygdala, also located in the limbic system, is larger in boys and is responsible for fight or flight.

Therefore, successful teachers or coaches are usually the ones who combine a mixture of lessons associated with movement and stationary contemplation to satisfy both types of learners.

Another area of intense failure with the student's brain can occur with weak test-taking skills, particularly with the student who expresses his intelligence *kinesthetically*. Such students may fail during the test-taking experience because their bodies are placed in a sitting or stationary situation. Again, sitting during a test situation can create an unnatural feeling in the amygdala or limbic system, particularly for boys, which can create test anxiety. On the playground or on the athletic field such individuals use their body (movement) and brain simultaneously for peak performance.

However, sitting at a desk can affect critical learning brain centers such as the cerebellum, which is linked to the somatosensory area of the cerebral cortex, etc. One simple strategy is to allow the test taker to stand up during the test or to take frequent breaks to ground anxiety or again tap into the cerebellum. Another strategy is for the student to write a short letter (fifteen minutes) about her fears of test taking before taking the test. This has shown to improve test performance (*Journal of Science*, 2012). For younger students teachers can have students draw their feelings on paper before taking the test, such as with state mandated testing.

Moreover, studies have shown that students who used *cursive writing* scored higher on the SATs than those who printed (College Board, 2010).

Also, students learn better if conditions are arranged so that they have to make *errors*. In other words, students who take tests on material before studying it remember the information better and longer than those who study without pretesting (Finn et al., 2010).

Whatever strategy you choose, it is imperative that you address the cognitive and emotional factors of fear failure along with the more obvious strategies such as specialized tutors, increased study times, conferences with teachers, etc.

Chapter 49

When Sleep Affects a Student's Learning Brain

Educators need to address the effect circadian rhythms and/or REM sleep patterns have on student performance. Circadian rhythms operate out of the hypothalamus, which regulates the fluctuations of the student's bodily functions such as breathing, digestion, temperature, hormone concentration, etc. According to brain scientists there are certain periods of time when students learn more efficiently than during other periods.

A student's circadian rhythm defines when he has his highest ability to focus and absorb new material. Interestingly, cognitive rhythms are about the same for the preadolescent and adult, but for adolescents, a group most susceptible to disrupted sleep patterns, this cognitive rhythm occurs one hour later.

Most teachers are acutely aware of the 8 a.m. to 12 a.m. time block as a high learning period, when students' circadian rhythms are considered best for learning. However, 12 p.m. to 4:00 p.m. is the weakest time for learning potential. From 4 p.m. and on, student circadian rhythms regroup and move back to high points of learning potential (Sousa, 2005).

Unfortunately, there is a *Catch-22* to all of this, and that has to do with REM (rapid eye movements) or sleep. Students should experience six REM periods over the course of a nine-hour sleep. Therefore, the adolescent would have to go to bed at 10:00 p.m. and get up at 7 a.m. to satisfy the need for six REM cycles. The selling point is that with each REM cycle, we have *greater capacity* for memory consolidation. In short, what your student learned during the day (working memory) has a greater chance of being encoded or stored into long-term memory during REM sleep cycles.

Moreover, memory consolidation occurs more easily when the brain is not preoccupied with external stimuli which occurs during REM sleep and which also supports your student's circadian rhythms. This may explain why people who review important information before going to sleep are likely to remember that information the next day on a test (Sousa, 2005).

A major dilemma? Parents cannot expect students to simply retire to bed early. According to medical researchers, the adolescents' late sleep cycles are part of the maturation of the endocrine system. From the onset of puberty until late teen years, the brain chemical, melatonin, which is responsible for sleepiness, is secreted from about 11 p.m. until around 8 a.m., nine hours later!

This secretion is based on human circadian rhythms and is fixed. In other words, typical youth are not able to fall asleep much before 11 p.m., and their brains will remain in sleep mode until about 8 a.m., regardless of what time they go to bed (CAREI— 1996). Classes in many high schools with early start times will cause students to rise earlier to get to school. Twenty percent of students sleep through the first two hours of school because their brains and/ or bodies are still in the REM sleep mode. The loss of adequate sleep each night also results in a *sleep debt* for most teens. In extreme cases, the student may even develop a clinical disorder called *delayed sleep phase disorder*.

However, data from a research study in the Minneapolis public schools showed that there was a significant reduction in school dropout rates, less depression, drug use and higher grades when they addressed students' REM sleep and circadian rhythms (Wehlstrom, 1996).

For starters, educators need to look more closely at academic classes during the peak and down time hours, particularly classes that allow students to move about in the afternoons. The second suggestion is that schools, especially high schools, should start later to support both circadian rhythms and REM (rapid eye movements) sleep as demonstrated by the Minneapolis Public Schools Study (1998).

Chapter 50

What Students Think?

Studies have shown that only 35 percent of high school seniors demonstrate the ability to think abstractly or can entertain three plus ideas at one time (Kuhn et al, 1977). Abstract thinkers can understand the US Constitution, basic algebra, and beyond. Reasons given by researchers for the low student percentage might be due to a preoccupation with grades or simply memorizing information rather than truly understanding its content.

One strategy that could stimulate greater thinking skills with students and recommended by Edward d' Bono's excellent book called *de Bono's Thinking Course* (Facts on File, 1998) is called the PMI method. The PMI method is an attention directing tool and stands for *plus, minus, and interesting* and has shown to improve students' thinking skills, as well abstract thinking. In conducting a PMI, you deliberately direct the students' attention first toward the plus points, then toward the minus points, and finally toward the interesting points. This is done in a very deliberate and disciplined manner over a period of about two to three minutes in all.

Researchers asked a class of 30 ten- to eleven-year-olds if they should be paid $5 for going to school. Some of the students' plus points included the following: *you can buy more candy* or *you could save up for a bike!* The minus points ranged from *big kids could beat you up to get the money* or *parents would not give presents or pocket money*. The interesting points were less black and white and according to researchers seemed to produce higher order thinking with the students. Other answers included *you could see what kind of candy kids like,* or *you can donate the money to homeless animals.*

In addition, at the end of the exercise the class was asked again if students should be paid $5 for going to school. Whereas 30 out of 30 ten- to eleven-year-olds had previously liked the idea, it now appeared that twenty-nine out of thirty had completely reversed their view and now disliked the idea.

Moreover, teachers noticed that the class felt the PMI approach helped the students to step back and look at questions differently. Some students commented that their *interesting points* were not just black and white but more like gray, especially when you think of all the interesting ways to answer the question. Other students said *they felt smarter after they used the PMI thinking method,* or *that it works better when nobody can make up their mind!*

Introducing *interesting* as a third point to stimulate thinking helped the students to think outside the box and elicited more abstract thinking responses.

Researchers often refer to the PMI method as the *spectacle method,* like giving a nearsighted person the appropriate glasses so the person would be able to see things more clearly or have a different view of the situation. In other words, the actual thinking tools become the glasses allowing students to see more clearly. We then react to what we see.

Parents need to look for strategies or methods to help students to learn and express their true intelligence. Improving a student's thinking skills is another path toward school and life's successes. What needs to be asked is not what students think about the PMI method, but what do their parents think?

Chapter 51

Becoming Aware of Myths Surrounding Learning

With the school year in full force, it would make sense to eliminate some common myths about your student's learning brain.

Myth Number One: according to brain researchers most attempts to motivate students to *try harder* do not light up unused neural circuits; academic achievement does not improve by simply running up a neural volume switch (Tokuhama-Espinosa, 2011). Instead, researchers advocate that effective learning should be similar to the experience of the long distance runner: steady, consistent, etc.

In other words, *cramming* aka *trying hard* often backfires. Instead, students should employ a strategy called *distributive practice* for better results (Dunlosky et al., 2014). Distributive practice suggests that students should spread out study time or learning to support greater retention, which feeds into working memory and executive thinking.

Myth Number Two: left- and right-brain students learn differently. Brain scientists believe a purely rational left brain and/or artistic right brain is considered a fable. We use both sides of our brain for all cognitive functions.

One of the most complex brain activities students will be asked to learn is *reading mastery,* which touches multiple areas of the brain. First, visual processing begins when the eyes scan the letters of the printed word and the visual signals travel to the occipital lobe located in the back of the head. The word signals are decoded in an area on the left side of the temporal lobe, which separates it into basic sounds (phonemes). The auditory processing system sounds out the phonemes and the frontal lobe provides the meaning. Again, to identify a child as purely right or left brain does not do justice to the 100 billion neurons located in all portions of a student's brain.

Myth Number Three: you should speak only one language first before learning another language. This could confuse one language over another causing language to develop slowly. Different areas of the brain do not compete for resources. Children who learn two languages simultaneously gain better-generalized knowledge of language structure as a whole.

Myth Number Four: male and female brains differ in function which then dictates different learning abilities. According to brain researcher Tracy Tokuhama-Espinosa, *"the distinctive physiology may result in differences in the way their brains function. No research has demonstrated gender specific differences in how networks of neurons become connected when we learn new skills."* Further, if gender differences do appear, they are likely small and based on averages that will not be relevant to any specific individual.

A final myth is that each child has a particular learning style. But specific learning styles have not been validated in actual studies (*Mind, Brain and Education Science*, 2014). A child may appear to exhibit skills at one time of his life, but three or four years later that same skill may be judged as a weakness. The reasons are complex, but the important thing to know is that a child's strengths and weaknesses are not carved in stone. As time passes, the way a child learns best may change significantly.

Neuroscientist Dr. Uta Frith urges parents and educators to tread cautiously: she explains, *"There is a huge demand by the general public to have information about neuroscience for education. There is an enormous supply of untested, untried and not very scientific methods."*

Chapter 52

The Donut Hole in School Test Scores!

With mandated state testing looming on your students' horizon, why focus *only* on test score results when there are so many other factors that are never reported such as those parents, teachers, and students who give tireless energy for successful school achievement. Unfortunately, they are the unknowns, the unsung heroes lost in an aggregate of numbers called test scores. These unknowns are what I like to call the *donut hole* in test scores that are rarely if ever discussed.

For example, there is no mention of family dynamics such as divorce, separation, and single parent homes that can affect not only student performance and test scores but also teaching and parental styles. Studies have shown that the emotional stress caused by disruptive family issues can delay student learning and even social development.

Further, teachers can have in one class at least 50 percent of their students (national average) living in divorce, separated, or single parent and/or blended family homes. In fact, negative family dynamics is so powerful that teachers can usually *predict a year in advance* when parents are having marital problems simply by the child's school performance. Regardless of such distractions, many parents, teachers, and students persevere and still achieve high academic achievement, thanks to these unsung heroes or unknowns.

In addition, many students often live in two homes, spending three or four days a week in one home, the next three days in another home. Rather than critique this arrangement we should give praise to those parents who are simply trying to keep the family unit intact. Maintenance requires a tremendous amount of energy on all parties—different rules, different parenting styles, different stepparents, and so forth. For all intents and purposes, many students still exhibit high school achievement regardless of such distractions, thanks in great part to teachers, parents, and of course the effort by students that often goes unnoticed.

Economics (recession) can have a domino effect on school performance as well. For instance, when a parent loses a job, most often he loses financial stability, which creates added stress on himself and the family. Furthermore, loss of a job can mean possible relocation of the family. This could affect the child's school performance such as the loss of friends, his school, and bonding with teachers. And, there is always the never mentioned factor of teacher stress, watching *her students* stress over family changes and school transfers of students she has worked with closely for months, sometimes years.

Therefore, let's give praise to parents, teachers, and those students who, regardless of the circumstances or challenges, are successful in their school achievement; yet they never get the recognition they deserve because there is that *donut hole* in test scores that is rarely discussed.

Chapter 53

Humor and Student Intelligence

A prerequisite for any aspiring teacher should be a course in stand-up comedy. Imagine Mark Twain as a teacher to aspiring teachers? Better yet, find a teacher-comic to teach the class. Aspiring teachers would be lined up to register for such a course.

Some of the most effective teachers are often great storytellers or great humorists. More importantly, they also have expert knowledge in the subject matter they are teaching.

One little secret that brain scientists have known for some time is that humor is the brain's natural stimulant because it has shown to increase greater learning and intelligence. For example, connecting humor to a school lesson provides the student's brain with more oxygen and glucose (sugar), which are both essential brain fuel ingredients.

In addition to increased oxygen and glucose, humor secretes natural pain-killers called *endorphins* into the blood steam, which then stimulates *serotonin*, a feel good drug. Ask any long distance runner what he feels like after a run and he will usually talk about a runner's high, when in reality he really should be thanking the chemical serotonin for the change in body state. The euphoria a runner experiences could be what humor can do with classroom learning in the hands of the right teacher.

Moreover, humor unifies the body and mind, a learning experience that stimulates the cerebellum, seat of sensory/gross motor skills. Furthermore, endorphins stimulate the brain's frontal lobes, which support greater memory consolidation and focusing (Sousa, 2005).

Another important fact about humor is that it reduces stress or the chemical cortisol. Increased levels of cortisol in the bloodstream have shown to have a negative effect on cognitive functioning.

In addition, humor lowers one's blood pressure, which can change the entire energy of the class environment to one of a relaxed alertness. In other words, rather than a student mistrusting the learning experience, which only fuels the fight or flight mode of learning and intelligence, you could see a more trustful learner. This trust feeds into the brain's hippocampus, a major component of greater memory consolidation and long-term memory.

Finally, students are constantly being challenged with rules and laws, particularly during adolescence. Humor could make school rules more palatable because school would now energize even the most complacent and cynical learner. Bottom line: humor is a great learning tool that every college or university needs to incorporate into their education curricula. Just ask Mark Twain who connected humor to learning when he said, "*I never let my schoolin interfere with my education!*"

Chapter 54

Neurofeedback: How to Get into the Zone!

"It's a very strange feeling. It's as if time slows down and you see every-thing so clearly. You just know that everything about your technique is spot on. It just feels so effortless; it's almost as if you're floating across the track. Every muscle, every fiber, every sinew is working in complete har-mony and the end product is that you run fantastically well" (Mind Games, Grout and Perrin, 2006).

Being in the zone is every athlete's dream. For amateurs, it may happen only a few times in their athletic life. For professionals, it could be a constant; occurring each time their mind and body operate as one, allowing for the highest degree of athletic performance. In fact, the ability to tap into the zone might be the one factor that separates the superb athlete from the average athlete. The successful athlete can tap into the zone more frequently, whereas the average athlete cannot.

When an individual is in the zone, he experiences what could be termed relaxed concentration or the time period during which sensory and motor skills operate in perfect harmony. For professional athletes, the zone con-dition allows the game or competition to come to a crawl. The baseball becomes larger and moves more slowly. Every putt in golf is makeable. The same might be said of the surgeon in the operating room or CEO dealing with an intense business deal.

Some brain scientists describe the zone as functioning between acute awareness and/or energized focus. A person in the zone feels immersed in a state of single-minded fusion in the act of performing or learning. He can access the zone by inducing gamma wave states. Gamma wave states show up as bursts of activity at 40 Hz every ten to fourteen seconds. Or they may show up as bursts of the famous alpha wave, at 10 Hz.

Both are markers for the desired state. We all function with these same frequencies. However, great athletes can get into an expanded gamma or focused gamma state more quickly and probably more intensely than average players of a similar skill level. Monks arrive in their zone during meditation.

An important brain area associated with the zone is our brain's left hemisphere, which represents our critical side, particularly when we experience failure. When performance is inconsistent, the brain tends to react both cognitively and emotionally. At the cognitive level, the left brain tries its best to assert control. At the emotional level, the right brain anticipates repeat failure and reacts accordingly. Both strategies by the brain are disruptive of the state of *being in the zone*, and therefore may be counterproductive.

What characterizes the *flow state* is a kind of *automaticity*. The right things just seem to happen effortlessly and without a lot of forethought. If, in anticipation of failure, the left hemisphere grabs the reins, it may very well "over-think" the situation. And if the right hemisphere grabs the reins, the emotional turmoil may well short-circuit higher order thinking and executing. Lost in this process is the *unitary* quality, the effortless fusion of right- and left-hemisphere function that characterizes *being in the zone*.

We are beginning to understand the neural circuitry that underlies these marvelous functional capacities. We are beginning to understand how disruptive our fear circuitry can be to our functional status and how our *executive function* can be undermined. Also, we are beginning to understand how the smooth integration of our left and right hemispheres is reflected in higher gamma and alpha amplitudes, which is the key to our optimum performance.

Athletes use meditation and creative visualization, and as we know, performance enhancing drugs (PED) to improve performance and/or to get into the zone. Unfortunately, meditation and visualization have proved to produce only limited success with athletes. (As for PED, there are multiple problems that need no further explaining). Fortunately, one successful non-invasive strategy that can promote gamma- and alpha-wave states is called neurofeedback.

Interestingly, neurofeedback has also proved to be highly successful with ADHD children who have a serious problem focusing and almost always are in a constant stage of over-arousal. Neurofeedback has been supported by the American Association of Pediatrics as having Level1 efficacy (top ranking) in application to ADHD.

How does neurofeedback work to produce a zone-like experience? Training generally consists of placing a couple of electrodes on the scalp and one or two electrodes on the earlobes. Then EEG equipment provides real-time, instantaneous audio and visual feedback to the subject about his brainwave activity. No electrical current is put into the brain. The brain's electrical activity is simply relayed to the computer. Ordinarily we cannot reliably influence our brainwave patterns because we lack awareness of them.

However, when we can see a representation of our brainwave activity on a computer screen a small fraction of a second after they occur, it gives us the ability to influence and change them through a process of operant conditioning. We are now literally able to recondition and retrain the brain. At first, the changes are short-lived, but the changes gradually become more enduring and with continuing feedback, coaching, and practice, improved brain functioning can usually be trained in most people, and the changes are enduring.

Electrode placements can be determined based on quantitative EEG brain mapping assessments, or in relation to areas of the brain associated with various functional roles in relationship to the International 10–20 System of Electrode Placement (*The Journal of the American Board of Sport Psychology*, Volume 1, 2007; Article #1).

The key to optimal athletic performance is understanding the nature of mind and body. For instance, Olympic Beach Volleyball champion Kerri Walsh-Jennings incorporated neurofeedback into her training routine for the Olympics. The Canadian Olympic team used neurofeedback extensively in the 2010 Olympics in Vancouver. Alexandre Bilodeau, the Canadian men's mogul champion, credited his gold medal to neurofeedback. He used it effectively to relax between runs. Also, the NHL's Vancouver Canucks, after a twenty-year post-season drought, skated their way to a 2011 Stanley Cup championship.

The Italian National Soccer team kicked up their performance by using neurofeedback and took home the World Cup in 2006. Finally, star athletes from the NBA, NFL, LPGA, and PGA (Phil Mickelson) have turned to neurofeedback for that mental advantage that can move them above and beyond the competition (Admin, 2013).

Chapter 55

Restorative Justice or Zero Tolerance

Ex-president Obama's speech concerning the elimination of a zero tolerance discipline philosophy in American public schools is long overdue. Zero tolerance is a tool that became popular in the 1990s, supporting uniform and swift punishment for offenses such as truancy, smoking, or possession of a weapon. Violators could lose classroom time and even be saddled with a criminal record.

The recommendations encouraged schools to ensure that all school personnel be trained in classroom management, *conflict resolution*, and approaches to de-escalate classroom disruptions. According to Attorney General Holder, *"the problem with a zero tolerance philosophy is that it often stems from well-intentioned zero-tolerance policies that too often injected the criminal justice system into the resolution of problems."*

Police have become a more common presence in American schools since the shootings at Columbine High School in 1999. However, what was missing from Obama's anti-zero tolerance presentation is the promotion of a more concrete approach, which could replace the old policy with restorative justice.

For example, statistics from one study describes the effectiveness of restorative justice on recidivism, the inability for those imprisoned to avoid future crime. In the first year, the restorative justice offenders had a recidivism rate of 15 percent compared to 38 percent for the probation group. In the second year the respective rates were 28 percent and 54 percent and by the third year the rates were 35 percent and 66 percent.

Brain scientists know the positive effects restorative justice can have on negative behavior, particularly with the adolescent's brain. Again, one major difference between zero-tolerance and restorative justice programs is that the dialogue is a face-to-face discussion about a problem. Face-to-face meetings stimulate the brain's hippocampus, which stimulates higher centers of the brain, potentially leading to rational thinking. Conversely, zero tolerance is based on law and order or rules that are set up by authority figures, using punishment to obtain adherence.

Therefore, the next time someone suggests using restorative justice versus zero tolerance in our schools, one can turn to the Colorado High School that has shown a great deal of success using restorative justice as their principal discipline policy. This Colorado High School, which has 75 percent of students qualifying for free and/or reduced lunches, showed a dramatic decrease in school violence after it enacted restorative justice as a form of discipline.

The school progressed from a high of 263 physical violence incidences in the 2007–2008 school year down to 31 for 2013–2014! Further, the restorative justice program at the Colorado High School has shown not only decreased suspension rates, anywhere from 40 to 80 percent, but has also resulted in a nearly 50 percent drop in absenteeism and a 60 percent decrease in tardiness. In short, the reason the Colorado restorative justice program works is simply because restorative justice is a more evolutionary/rational approach than zero tolerance.

Chapter 56

In Praise of Teaching

Many of the problems affecting a student's ability to learn can be traced to today's home environment. For example, yesterday's home environment was quieter and some might say even boring when compared to today's home environments. Parents and children did a great deal more talking and reading. Studies show that today's parents spend about twenty minutes of quality time with their children daily. Talking and reading stimulates the limbic system and the child's hippocampus, seat of emotional relationships, which can lead to greater intelligence, memory consolidation (episodic), and greater focusing skills.

Moreover, the family unit was more stable, often eating meals together; thus, allowing parents and children to actually discuss the day's activities. Family stability stimulates organization and predictability and supports the frontal lobes or executive centers of the brain, another necessary ingredient for greater learning potential and intelligence.

Also, TV was in a common area and controlled by adults. What children watched was actually monitored. Today's child on average will witness 200,000 violent acts and 16,000 murders by eighteen years of age. One study, tracking more than 700 adolescents into adulthood, found that young people who were watching one to three hours of television daily were almost four times more likely to commit violently aggressive acts later in life than those who watched less than an hour of TV a day.

Family units are not as stable. That is, about 50 percent of marriages end in divorce, a statistic that has remained consistent over the past decade. Studies show that a child who experiences a divorce or separation loses almost a year of school learning. In fact, teachers can actually predict a year in advance when a couple will divorce, simply by the school behavior of a particular student. Lastly, this study does not measure the psychological factors that can have lifelong effects on learning potential.

Furthermore, less time to form positive family relationships can delay students from experiencing higher stages of moral development (conforming to family rules), which affects discernment of right/wrong behavior.

Dietary habits have changed along with home cooking. In the past decade childhood obesity has increased substantially. With this increase in obesity at young ages has come early onset of puberty for girls. That is, 10 percent of white, 15 percent of Latino, and 23 percent of Afro-American girls are reaching puberty by age seven. For boys it is the opposite. Obesity affects self-esteem, which can affect a boy's learning potential and intelligence as well, causing later maturation.

In addition, additives in food can cause hyperactivity (ADHD), which affects classroom focusing ability, as well as behavioral problems.

Electronic media surrounds students: cell phones, iPods, TV, movies, video games, computers, etc. Teens spend nearly seventeen or more hours a week on the Internet and fourteen or more hours a week watching TV. The many hours devoted to electronics can affect sleep, as well as the student's classroom focusing ability. Adolescents need at least eight to nine hours of sleep or six REM cycles (rapid eye movements) of sleep for the day's school learning to be effectively transmitted to long-term storage and memory consolidation. Also, lack of sleep can cause a more serious problem, DSD (delayed sleep disorder), which carries over to classroom learning and focusing skills.

Finally, this addiction to electronics feeds into our novelty seeking brains. Dopamine, a neural transmitter often called *the gotcha* chemical, demands more and more stimulation, which can affect a student's classroom attention span. *I am bored*, a common sentence uttered by teens could be no more than their novelty seeking brain demanding more dopamine. Lastly, when students' brains are not getting enough stimulation, this lack of activity can motivate students to turn to other stimulants such as ecstasy or amphetamines, which will feed the student's dopamine seeking brain as well.

Teachers are more educated and well trained than ever before. Yet, today's teachers are being judged on yesterday's student home environments, which have dramatically changed a student's ability to learn and a teacher's ability to teach. Bottom line—education is the only profession that is asked to change the human brain on a daily basis (Sousa, 2005).

Chapter 57

Common Core Standards and the Learning Brain

With the advent of *common core standards*, many teachers are trying to decipher how it will impact their students' retention skills. In other words, one of the greatest challenges for most students is the ability to retain information, particularly, when there is a curriculum change, which can affect teaching methods. For example, a study conducted in the sixties by the NTL, National Training Laboratories, studied the effect of different teaching methods on learning retention.

The study is still relevant today. NTL devised a learning pyramid or the percentage of new learning that students could recall after twenty-four hours. The ability for students to recall information after twenty-four hours is defined as long-term storage and is critical to school success.

A study in 2005 by Moore showed that after three days, learning retention was lowest, only 10 percent with classroom lectures, but higher, 20 percent, when lectures consisted of demonstration. The percentages from the original 1960 study were rounded to the nearest 5 percent and again proved to be frighteningly reflective to studies of this time period.

The 1960 study defined lecture at the top of the pyramid or an average learning retention of only 5 percent after twenty-four hours. Anyone who has sat through the lecture format knows that retention involves verbal processing with little active participation or mental rehearsal. Moreover, with the lecture format, the teacher verbalizes and the student listens just enough to convert the teacher's auditory output to written notes.

Further, rote rehearsal predominates as auditory information moves onto the notebook (Sousa, 2005). Unfortunately, there is no elaborative rehearsal, a means to develop meaning, and thereby create an opportunity for the brain to encode information, which is why, information is lost for most students. Ironically, regardless of the lack of learning retention with the lecture format, lecture actually predominates most teaching programs in high school and college.

The hook for the lecture format is that it allows a lot of information to be presented in a short period of time, which could be a response by teachers to the shortened school year. But that would be another topic for future discussion.

Let's examine the rest of the sixties study pyramid. We have learned that the average percentage of retention after twenty-four hours for each of the instruction methods was verbal processing at 5 percent for lecture and for reading at 10 percent. Next are verbal and visual processing or auto visual, 20 percent; demonstration 30 percent and discussion group 50 percent. Practice by doing reached a 70 percent retention level, and finally teaching others as immediate use of learning hit 90 percent retention. The doing format implies the necessity to use new information immediately.

When you explain, you learn, which is why cooperative learning groups and even hands-on programs might explain why underachieving students often succeed in programs that are more hands on. In short, our studies have shown for decades that the best way to retain learned material is to prepare to teach it. Whoever explains learns (Sousa, 2005).

Of course no one teaching method is best for all students, all the time. If Common Core Standards allow for students to be actively engaged in learning, it will be a win-win situation for all involved.

Chapter 58

Poverty and Children's Brain Development!

A recent newspaper article explaining that the *eight richest men* in the world have more wealth than half of the world's population motivated me to research poverty rates and their effect on children's learning brains.

According to official poverty statistics, 22.7 percent of families in California were classified as not having enough resources to make ends meet in 2014. This is down from 2013 (23.5 percent), but well above the recent low in 2007 (17.3 percent). The question remains: what effect does poverty have on children's brain development and school learning, as well as long range problems concerning further employment and economic security (Public Policy Institute of California, 2014).

Researcher, Sean Reardon at Stanford University, recently completed an analysis showing that children in California school districts with high levels of poverty score an average of four grade levels lower on tests in reading and math, far below peers from the most affluent districts. Further, kids born to low-income families have a greatly reduced chance of getting a college degree than children born to a high-income family, affecting economic and career opportunities (Gabrielli & Bunge, 2017).

Moreover, an MIT study compared the cortex's (brain's executive thinking) thickness among fifty-eight eighth grade students from lower income versus higher income families. The results of the 2015 study showed that the lower income group had a thinner cortex in many areas of the brain. For all students, regardless of income, a thicker cortex was associated with better scores on statewide reading and math tests. Lastly, the study related family income, brain anatomy, and education achievement to higher school achievement.

Interestingly, researchers also considered another factor concerning a reduced cortex. That is, a reduced cortex may simply be due to the negative effects of impoverished environments or what researchers described as a "protective adaptation to such environments" (Gabrieli & Bunge, 2017). In other words, "accelerated thinning could diminish the influence of negative experiences on the developing brain." In short, the researchers theorized that preventing the brain from being shaped by negative school experiences over the course of many years could be a cause of what researchers describe as an "adaptive evolutionary response" or thinning of the cortex.

There are a number of ways researchers suggest how to improve learning for disadvantaged children. First, it can come from prevention of negative impacts, such as sleep, nutrition, and then remediation or cognitive and academic skill development and for parents in areas such as finances, career development, and parenting strategies.

One approach is a program called Kids in Transition to School (KITS). The KITS program offers 24 sessions of therapeutic play for children, as well as an eight-session workshop for parents. The program addresses children's basic classroom skills (raising hands, taking turns, etc.) while their parents learn strategies about routines with children that encourage positive behavior. A follow-up study of the KITS program showed that nonverbal IQ and language skills increased (Gabrieli & Bunge, 2017).

Another program called "Tools of the Mind Curriculum" serves as an alternative to the traditional kindergarten. The curriculum focuses on building executive functions through "scaffolding play." Scaffolding play enables a child to solve a problem, carry out a task, or achieve a goal which is just beyond his or her abilities. In 2014, follow-up studies found this program to be especially beneficial to high poverty preschoolers.

Due to the ability of the brain to change, researchers see hope for disadvantaged children. The most successful programs will involve multiple, regular sessions that incorporate children, caregivers, and educators engaging in a range of skills in a diverse manner. However, the best approach would be public policies and societal changes that attempt to reduce child poverty and income inequality (Gabrieli & Bunge, 2017).

Chapter 59

Moral Remediation and Sports Should Be a Two-Way Street

Recently, several universities were charged with National Collegiate Athletic Association (NCAA) violations when football players were found to have received large sums of money and gifts—even prostitution, from overly enthusiastic alumni/patrons. In all, the dollar value of the money or gifts was extensive. The NCAA has yet to make a ruling on the degree of punishment for violators; however, some years ago, the most severe penalty ever passed down to a school for an NCAA violation was to Southern Methodist University (SMU)—their football program was canceled.

Such an action could never occur today—there are simply too many schools that regularly break NCAA rules; college football is big business—it raises big money for cash scrapped schools. Bottom line—taking gifts by an NCAA athlete, coach, etc. of any amount is against NCAA rules, yet it is done over and over again. Therefore, how do you control alumni/patrons whose bottom line is winning at all costs or do we disregard the messenger and center on athletes to help them not only to resist temptation, but to report unscrupulous individuals?

One proven method shown to raise an individual's level of moral development and which could be a panacea to college players susceptible to taking illegal gifts is Dr. Lawrence Kohlberg's theory of moral development. Over a three-year period, Kohlberg was able to lower the recidivism rate of juvenile offenders from a high of 33 percent to a low of 18 percent by conducting more development groups.

Specifically, by raising juvenile offender's moral reasoning, he was also able to help them develop a greater respect for law and order, which in turn helped lower the recidivism rate.

Kohlberg's theory is neither complicated nor difficult to implement, and which is why I advocate his theory as a strategy to helping college athletes who might be prone to accepting gifts from college alumni/patrons and/or breaking rules that could mean loss of a scholarship, an entire university team placed on probation, all because of a minority of individuals, including coaches and patrons whose bottom-line is winning at all costs. Kohlberg administered moral dilemmas to several groups of boys over a thirty-year period that defined six stages of moral development, and which was later altered to five stages. The key to Kohlberg theory is directly connected to cognition or how we think and/or moral judgment or how we deal with life's dilemmas, such as dishonest gift taking by college athletes.

An effective method to describe Kohlberg's theory is how we might teach math to elementary school children. In first grade, the child begins with basic addition (one operation), then from about second to fourth: addition, subtraction, multiplication with regrouping (two plus operations), and ultimately division (fourth/fifth grade) and three plus operations (divide, multiply, subtract, and bring down). The key is to teach math principles that are as close to the student's cognitive level as possible.

In other words, you do not teach first graders basic addition and next division—their brains are not ready to accommodate more than one operation! The same holds true for moral development; that is, most seven- to ten-year-olds judge the world in black and white, or fair versus unfair. In short, they are able to handle two operations or ideas at one time—theirs and yours.

As they move up the moral development ladder, they can take the perspective of more than two ideas or in our math example, division or three plus operations, be it family, school, society, etc. Again, the key is to introduce information slightly above the individual's level of thinking. Kohlberg was able to lower juvenile offenders' recidivism rates by stimulating a greater understanding or respect for rules and laws dictated by the group.

We can apply the same premise by our teaching of math example. Instead of seeing the world of rules as *fair versus unfair* (Kohlberg's stage 2—"Individualism and Exchange"), juvenile offenders could now think abstractly (Kohlberg's stage 3—*Good Interpersonal Relationships*) or take the perspective of the group or three plus operations.

First, Kohlberg assessed the offenders to find out their level of moral development; then challenged them with real-life moral dilemmas that were slightly higher than their level of moral development, which for most juvenile offenders was stage 2—*fair versus unfair*. In addition, when juvenile offenders gave answers that were at stage 2, he presented his point of view at stage 3, or again, slightly higher than their level of understanding.

Kohlberg was correct in believing that it is our brain's natural tendency to want to think at a higher level, which is why the juvenile offenders developed a greater respect for rules—*not fair versus unfair* but to conform to the group's rules or laws, which is society.

Apply this same example to athletes who broke NCAA rules by taking gifts and money and we begin to see why Kohlberg's theory could be a valuable strategy for changing the mindset of athletes who are prone to break rules. They see the world concretely or in black and white and follow rules based on what is fair versus unfair. For some athletes, it becomes particularly unfair when they see the money universities make on ticket sales, TV contracts, versus what they receive—a free ride, as well as the possibility of risking life and limb in a football game.

Moreover, such a mindset starts early in a gifted athlete's life. When young athletes are rewarded with gifts for their athletic performance as young adults they often are molded to think entirely at stage 2, and like those who took gifts and money are rooted in stage 2 moral reasoning—*fair versus unfair.*

And why stop with university athletes when professional athletes are also prone to low moral judgment. The Michael Vicks of the world might not have ever surfaced if each particular pro team developed a segment of their training before drafting or contracting with a high priced player by first assessing their moral judgment.

Fortunately, by using basic moral judgment assessments to determine an individual's moral stage and moral remediation similar to what Kohlberg implemented with juvenile offenders, most college or pro athletes who think at stage 2 can be moved to higher stages. The bottom line—are colleges and pro teams willing take the leap to moral remediation or are they content to stay the course and allow these players to fail? If this is the case then what moral stage are our universities and pro teams operating?

Chapter 60

When Choosing Wrong Answers Can Be Right

With tests always on the front burner for many students, new research suggests that unusual test-taking techniques can actually help students achieve higher performance. For example, most students are taught what is called "errorless learning" or to create study conditions that prevent errors. However, some researchers suggest a more unorthodox approach that can actually increase learning. For example, teachers might drill students consistently on the same multiplication problems, with very little delay between the first and second presentations of the problem, ensuring that the student gets the correct answer each time. Yet, according to researchers, the twist is that students who make mistakes will remember the mistakes and not learn the correct answers. Or will they learn it more slowly, if at all?

Researchers Roediger and Finn suggest that students learn better if conditions are actually arranged so that they have to make errors. They believe that *"students will remember things better and longer if they are given challenging tests that they are bound to fail."*

Moreover, psychologist Richland and associates (2009) also support the notion that trying and failing to retrieve answers can actually shape learning. *"Students who make unsuccessful attempts to answer test questions before receiving the correct answers remember the material better than if they studied the information."*

A study by psychologist Dr. Jeffrey Karpicke demonstrated that taking a memory test enhances later retention. In his two experiments students first studied prose passages. Then, one group took one of three immediate free recall tests, without feedback, while another group restudied the material the same number of times as the students who received the tests.

On tests given later, at two days and at one week, there was a substantial difference between the groups—students who had been tested remembered

around 60 percent of the material, whereas students who restudied remembered only about 40 percent of the material (Karpicke, 2009). The results
support the work of Richland (2009) that testing before learning can improve
later recall as well.

The key—rather than aiming for *errorless learning,* teachers should challenge their students to try to answer questions about a subject before they
study the material. Even if it is not used in the classroom, students can use
it on their own to improve their learning process (Roediger & Finn, 2009).

Researchers suggest additional techniques: *"students should look at the
questions in the back of each textbook chapter and try to answer them before
reading the chapter." If there are no questions, convert the section heading
to a question. If the section is "Pavlovian conditioning,"* students should ask
themselves what is Pavlovian conditioning. Then read the chapter and answer
the questions while reading it. When the chapter is finished, go back to the
question and try answering them again.

For any you miss, restudy that section of the chapter. Then wait a few days
and try to answer the questions again (restudying when you need to). Keep
this practice up for an entire course, and you will have learned and retained
the material, as well as being able to retrieve it long after you have left the
course (Roediger & Finn, 2009).

Our authors close by saying, *"there are general-purpose strategies that
work for any type of material, not just strategies for textbooks. By challenging ourselves to retrieve or generate answers, we can improve recall. When
you turn to Google for an answer, students can attempt to come up with the
answer on their own."*

And it doesn't matter if you get the answer wrong with self-testing during
study; the research suggests that the process is still useful, and more useful
than just studying alone. Bottom line, getting wrong answers supports learning as long as you retrieve the answers after.

Bibliography

Abuse, N. I. (2006). *Anabolic Steroid Abuse*. Washington, DC: US Department on Health and Human Services, National Institutes of Health.

American Academy of Pediatrics. (2012–2013). *Evidence-Based Child and Adolescent Psychosocial Interventions*. San Rafael, CA.

American Behavioral Scientist—Vol 48, Number 5, Jan. 01, 2005.

American For the Arts (2012). "Art students out perform Non-art Students on SAT (Average Points Better on SAT's by Arts Students). New York: College Board.

Anvari, S. H., Trainor, L. J., Woodside, J., & Levy, B. A. (2002, October). Relations among musical skills, phonological processing, and early Reading ability in preschool children. *Journal of Experimental Child Psychology*, 83, 111–30.

Baron-Cohen, S. (2003). *The Essential Difference: The truth About the Male and Female brain*. New York: Basic Books.

Barry, N., Taylor, J., & Walls, K. (2002). The role of the fine and performing arts in high school dropout prevention. In R. J. Deasy (ed.), *Critical Links: Learning in the Arts and Student Academic and Social Development* (74–75). Washington, D.C.: Arts Education Partnership.

BCNI - 96 Chapter 44, Abnormalities in Dopamine Transmission. U.K., 2013.

Bloom, B. S. (1976). *Human Characteristics and School Learning*. New York: McGraw-Hill.

Bohn, S. & Danielson, C. (2017). "Poverty in CA - Just the Facts." Sacramento, CA: PPIC Public Policy Institute of California.

Bonta, J., Wallace-Capretta, S., Rooney, J., & McAnoy, K. (2002). An outcome evaluation of a restorative justice alternative to incarceration. *Contemporary Justice Review*, 5, 319–38.

Brannon, E. J., & Van Der Walle, G. (2001). Ordinal numerical knowledge in young children. *Cognitive Psychology*, 43, 53–81.

Bratton, et al. (2005) "The Efficacy of Play Therapy with Children." Professional Psychology: *Research and Practice*, 36(4), 376–90. APA Psyc. NET. Washington, D.C.

Buckley, W. "Estimated Prevalance of Anabolic Steroid Use Among H.S. Seniors." *Research Gate*. Jan. 1998. Vol. 26. No. 23. Berlin, Germany.

Burton, J. M., Horowitz, R., & Abeles, H. (2000). Learning in and through the arts: The question of transfer. *Studies in Art Education*, 41, 228–57.

Butterworth, B. (1999). *What Counts: How Every Brain Is Hardwired for Math*. New York: Free Press.

Buzan, T. (1989). *Use Both Sides of Your Brain* (3rd ed.). New York: Penguin.

Buzzell, K. (1998). *The Children of Cyclops: The Influence of Television Viewing on the Developing Human Brain*. San Francisco, CA: Association of Waldorf Schools of North America.

Cahill, L. (2005, May). His brain, her brain. *Scientific American*, 292, 40–47. New York.

Calvin, W. (2004). *A Brief History of the Mind: From Apes to Intellect and Beyond*. New York: Oxford University Press.

Carter, T., Hardy, C. A., & Hardy, J. C. (2001, December). Latin vocabulary acquisition: An experiment using information-processing techniques of chunking and imagery. *Journal of Instructional Psychology*, 28, 225–28.

Chapman, C. (1993). *If the ShoeFfits: Developing the Multiple Intelligences Classroom*. Thousand Oaks, CA: Corwin Press.

Childwise (2015). *Research Highlights for Children's Public Safety:* #84. New York.

Chugani, H. T. (1998). A critical period of brain development: Studies of cerebral glucose utilization with PET. *Preventive Medicine*, 27, 184–88.

Cooper, H. (2003–2005) "Summer learning Loss: The Problems and Some Solutions." *Eric Digest*. Champaign, IL.

Cowan, N. (2001). The magical number 4 in short-term memory: A reconsideration of mental storage capacity. *Behavioral and Brain Sciences*, 24. Available online at www.bbsonline.org/documents.

Cozolino, L. (2017). The Neuroscience of Psychotherapy. *Healing the Social Brain*. New York. W.W. Norton and Company, Inc.

Deans, Emily, "Iron, Dopamine and ADHD," *Psychology Today* **February** 2015.

Deans, E. "ADHD." *Psychology Today*. Nov. 2015. New York.

De Bono, E. (1985). *de'Bono's Thinking Course*. New York: Facts on File.

Diamon, M., & Hopson, J. (1998). *Magic Trees of the Mind: How to Nurture Your Child's Intelligence, Creativity, and Healthy Emotions from Birth Through Adolescence*. New York: Dutton.

Delisio, E. (2010) *Education World*. Colchester, CT.

Dewey, G. et al. (1987). "Characteristics of Adolescents Charged with Homicide: Review of 72 Cases." Vol. 5, Issue 1, pp. 11–23. *Behavioral Sciences: The Law*, Medford, MA.

Droz, M., & Ellis, L. (1996). *Laughing While Learning: Using Humor in the Classroom*. Longmont, CO: Sopris West.

Druckerman, P. (2012). Bringing up Be'Be'. New York: Penguin Press.

Dunckley, V. (2015). *Reset Your Child's Brain: A Four-Week Plan to End Meltdowns, Raise Grades, and Boost Social Skills by Reversing the Effects of Electronic Screen-Time*. Navato, CA: New World Library.

Dunlosky, J., & Rawson, K. A. (2005). Why does rereading improve metacomprehension accuracy? Evaluating the levels-of-disruption hypothesis for the rereading effect. *Discourse Processes*, 40, 37–56.

Dunlosky, J. et al. (2014). "Improving Students' Learning With Effective Learning Techniques: Promising Directions." From Cognitive and Educational Psychology. *Psychological Science in the Public Interest*. 14(1), 4–58. Thousand Oaks, CA: Sage Publications.

Dweck, C. (April, 2015) The Secret to Raising Smart Kids. *Scientific American*. Washington, D.C.

Education Source. (2012). *Understanding school discipline in California: Perceptions and practice*. Retrieved at http://bit.ly/10ejXD4.

Edutopia—*What Works in Education* (2016). George Lucas Educational Foundation: USA.

Edwards, L. (2003). Writing instruction in kindergarten: Examining an emerging area of research for children with writing and reading difficulties. *Journal of Learning Disabilities*, 36(2), 136–48.

Environmental Health Perspective. Bisphenol A: 2007–2011. Triable Park, NC: US Department of Health and Human Services: Research.

Epub. (2011, May 13). Bisphenol A: An endocrine disruptor with widespread exposure and multiple intelligence. *Rubin BS1 Cognitive Processes*. Thousand Oaks, CA: Corwin Press.

Erickson, E. (1968). *Identity Youth and Crisis*. New York: W.W. Norton.

Evans, K. R. (2013). Doing time in ISS: A performance of school discipline. In R. Gabriel & J. N. Lester (eds.), *Performances of Research: Critical Issues in K-12Eeducation*. New York: Peter Lang.

Evans, K. R., & Lester, J. N. (2012). Zero tolerance: Moving the conversation forward. *Intervention in Schools and Clinics*, 48(2), 108–14.

Evans, K. R. & Lester, J. N. (2013). Restorative justice in education: What we know so far. *Middle School Journal*, 44(5), 57–63.

Farrell-Kirk, R. (2007, February). *Tips on Understanding and Encouraging Your Child's Artistic Development*. June 10, 2008.

Ferguson, L. (May, 2017). Benefits of Reading to Spot. Tuffs Now. Communing School of Vet Medicine, Tuffs University. Boston, MA.

Finn, et al. "Four Principals of Memory Improvement: A guide to Improving Learning Efficiency." *The International Journal of Creativity and Problem Solving*. 21(2011) (1) 7–15. Daega, Korea.

Fisch, S. M., Truglio, R.T., & Cole, C.F. (1999). The impact of *Sesame Street* on preschool children: A review and synthesis of 30 years' research. *Media Psychology*, *1*, 165–190. Boston: MA. Hogrefe Publishing Corp.

Fiske, R. D. (ed.). (1999). *Champions of Change: The impact of the Arts on Learning*. Washington, DC: President's Committee on the Arts and the Humanities.

Gabreelli, J. & Bundge, S. (2017). "The Story of Poverty." *Scientific American Mind* 28, 54–61. Washington D.C.

Gable, S. (2000). *Creativity in Young Children*. University of Missouri Extension. Downloaded on June 10, 2008.

Gaddes, W. (1985). *Learning Disabilities and Brain Function—A Neuropsychological Approach* (2nd ed.). New York: Springer Verlag.

Gardner, H. (1983). *Frames of the Mind—The Theory of Multiple Intelligences*. New York: Basic Books.

Gazzaniga, M. (2008). *Learning, Arts, and the Brain*. New York: Dana Press.

Geller & Walker. (2012). BPA BOMBSHELL: *Industry Database Reveals 16,000 Foods with Toxic Chemical in Packaging BFA. Action Plan*. EPA—US Environmental Protection Agency.

Gladwell, M. (2008). *Outliers: The Story of Success*. New York: Little, Brown Co.

Goldberg, E. (2001). *The Executive Brain: Frontal Lobes and the Civilized Mind*. New York: Oxford Press.

Goleman, D. (1995). *Emotional Intelligence: Why It Can Matter More Than I.Q.* New York: Bantam.

Gomez, M. (2010). *Art Therapy Helps Children Cope with Tragedy*. WCBS-TV, Channel 2, New York.

Gurian Institute (2015). Gurian Institute - Chandler, AZ.

Grout, J., & Perrin, S. (2006). *Mind Games: Inspirational Lessons from the World's Finest Sports Stars*. Washington D.C.: Capstone.

Haberman, C. (2016). "The Unintended Consequences of Taking a Hard line on School Discipline." *New York Times*. New York.

Harms, W. "Writing About Worries Eases Anxiety and Improves Test Performance." Jan, 2011. University of Chicago News.

Hallam, S. (2002). *The effects of background music on studying*. In R. J. Deasy (ed.), *Critical Links: Learning in the Arts and Student Academic and Social Development* (74–75). Washington, D.C.: Arts Education Partnership.

Hallam, S. (2005). *Enhancing Learning and Motivation Through the Life Span*. London: Institute of Education, University of London.

Hallam, S., & Prince, V. (2000). *Research into Instrumental Music Services*. London: Department for Education and Employment.

Hamann, D., Bourassa, R., & Aderman, M. (1990). *Creativity and the arts. Dialogue in Instrumental Music Education*, 14, 59–68.

Hamann, D., Bourassa, R., & Aderman, M. (1991). Arts experiences and creativity scores of high school students. *Contribution to Music Education*, 14, 35–47.

Harland, J., Kinder, K., Lord, P., Stott, A., Schagen, I., & Haynes, J. (2000). *Arts Education in Secondary Schools: Effects and Effectiveness*. London: NFER/The Arts Council of England, RSA.

Hart, L. (1983). *Human Brain and Human Learning*. New York: Longman.

Hawkins, J., & Blakeslee, S. (2004). *On Intelligence*. New York: Times Books.

Hetland, L. (2000a, Fall). Listening to music enhances spatial-temporal reasoning: Evidence for the "Mozart Effect." *Journal of Aesthetic Education*, 34, 105–48.

Hetland, L. (2006b) Learning to make music enhances spatial reasoning. *Journal of Aesthetic Education, 34(3/4), Special Issue, The Arts and Academic Achievement: What the evidence shows* (Autumn–Winter, 2000), 179–238.

Holland, J. (1993). SDS Personality and vocational interests: The relation of Holland's six interest dimensions to five robust dimensions of personality. Gottfredson, Gary D.; Jones, Elizabeth M.; Holland, John L. *Journal of Counseling Psychology*, 40(4), 518–24.

Hull, J. Center for Public Education (2011). "Time in school: How Does the US Compare?" *Center for Public Education*. Alexandria, VA.

The Endocrine Society (2009). "Endocrine Disrupting Chemicals: Hormone Science to Health." Chevy Chase, MD.

The International 10–20 System of Electrode Placement. *The Journal of the American Board of Sport Psychology Vol. 1–2007; Article #1*. Hammond, D.C.

Karpicke, J. (2016) "A Powerful Way to Improve Learning and Memory. *American Psychological Association*. Washington, D.C.

Keane, J. (2006). *The Big Book of Children's Reading Lists*. Westport, CT: Library Unlimited.

Kim, J. S., & Quinn, D. M. (2013). The effects of summer reading on low-income children's literacy achievement from Kindergarten to Grade 8: A meta-analysis of classroom and home interventions. *Review of Educational Research*, 83(3), 386–431.

Kimura, D. (1992, September). Sex differences in the brain. *Scientific American*, 267, 119–24.

Kohlerg, L. (1981). *Kohlberg, Lawrence—Essays on Moral Development, I: The Philosophy of Moral Development: Moral Stages and the Idea of Justice*. San Francisco, CA: Harper & Row.

Kuhn, D., Langer, J., Kohlberg, L., & Haan, N. S. (1977). The development of formal operations. in logical and moral judgment. *Genetic Psychology Monographs*, 95, 97–188.

Lawson, A. E. & Wollman, W. T. (1976). Encouraging the Transition from Concrete to Formal Cognitive Functioning – An Experiment. *Journal of Research in Science*. Wiley Online Library.

LeBoutillier, N., & Marks, D. F. (2003, February). Mental imagery and creativity: A meta-analytic review study. *British Journal of Psychology*, 94, 29–44.

Lewin, T. "Perfect's New Profile, Warts and All." Sept. 2006. New York Times.

Lewis, M. (2003). *Money Ball*. New York: W.W. Norton and Company.

Loomans, D., & Kolberg, K. (1993). *The Laughing Classroom: Everyone's Guide to Teaching with Humor and Play*. New York: H. J. Kramer.

Macquire, E. A., Frith, D. C., & Morris, R. G. M. (1999, October). The functional neuroanatomy of comprehension and memory: The importance of prior knowledge. *Brain*, 122, 1839–50.

Marshall, et al. "The effects of fathers on father figures on child behavioral problems in families referred to Child Protective Services." *Research Gate*. Vol. 6, Number 45. Nov. 2001.

Mayo Clinic Staff. "Performance Enhancing Drugs: Know the Risks." Oct. 2015. Foundation for Medical Ed. and Research, Mayo Clinic. Rochester, MN.

Mind, Brain, and Education Science. Tokuhama-Espinosa, T. W. W. Norton, 2010; "*Understanding the Brain: The Birth of a Learning Science*." OECD, 2007; OECD Educational Ministerial Meeting, November 4–5, 2010 New York.

Millman, R. P. (2005, June). Excessive sleepiness in adolescents and young adults: Causes, consequences, and treatment strategies. *Pediatrics*, 115, 1774–86.

Mischel, W., Shoda, Y. & Rodriguez, M. L. (1989). Delay of gratification in children. Science, 244(4907), 933–37. Washington, D.C.

Montessori, M. (2008). *The Montessori Method*. Radford, VA: Wilder Publication.

Muftuler, L. T., Bodner, M., Shaw, G. L., & Nalcioglu, O. (1999). fMRI of Mozaart effect using auditory stimuli. Abstract presented at the 7th meeting of the International Society for Magnetic Resonance in Medicine, Philadelphia.

Myers, J. (1997). *Our Stolen Future: Are We Threatening Our Fertility, Intelligence and Survival?* New York: Plume Publishing.

National Reading Panel (NRP). (2000). *Teaching Children to Read: An Evidence-based Assessment of the Scientific Research Literature and Its Implications for Reading Instruction*. Washington, D.C.: National Institute of Child Health and Human Development.

Northwestern University. "Diagnosis of ADHD on the Rise." *Science Daily*. 19 March, 2012.

Orenstein, P. (1994). *Schoolgirls: Young Women, Self-Esteem and the Confidence Gap*. New York: Doubleday.

Ornstein, R., & Thompson, R. (1984). *The Amazing Brain*. Boston: Houghton Mifflin.

Pearce, J. (1986). *Magical Child*. New York: Bantam.

Piaget, J. (1932). *The Moral Judgment of the Child*. New York: The Free Press.

Pinker, S. (2002). *The Blank Slate: The Modern Denial of Human Nature*. New York: Viking.

Pilcher, H. "Brain Machine Interfaces." 431, 993–96. Nature Oct. 2004.

Poldrack, R. (2009). *Russell Poldrack: May I Have Your Attention? The Brain, Multitasking and Information Overload*. Project Information Literacy.

Poldrack, R. (2011). *Multitasking: The Brain Seeks Novelty*. Austin, TX: University of Texas.

Rabkin, N., & Redmond, R. (2004). *Putting the Arts in the Picture: Reframing Education in the 21st Century*. Chicago: Columbia College.

Raths, J. (2002, Autumn). Improving instruction. *Theory into Practice*, 41, 233–37.

Reay, D. (2001). "Spice girls", "nice girls", "girlies", and "tomboys": Gender discourses, Girls' cultures and femininities in the primary classroom. *Gender and Education*, 13(2), 153–67.

Remer, H. et al. (1995). A quasi-experimental study. The effect of schooling on the development of fluid and crystallized intelligence. Elsevier, Inc. 21(3), Nov–Dec, 279–96.

Restak, R. M. (2001). *The Secret Life of the Brain*. Washington, D.C.: Dana Press.

Restak, R. M. (2003). *The New Brain: How the Modern Age Is Rewiring Your Mind*. New York: Rodale.

Richland, L. (2009). *Pub. Med*. National Institutes of Health. Washington, D.C.

Roberts, P., & Kellough, D. (2003). *A Guide for Developing Interdisciplinary Thematic Units* (3rd ed.). Englewood Cliffs, NJ: Prentice Hall.

Robertson, R. (2007, July/August). The meaning of marks: Understanding and nurturing young children's writing development. *Child Care Exchange*, 176, 40–44.

Roediger, H. and Finn, B. (2009). "Getting it Wrong: Surprising Tips on How to Learn." *Scientific American Mind*. Washington, D.C.

Roediger, H. & Finn, B. (2010, March/April) "The Pluses of getting it Wrong." *Scientific American Mind*. New York, N.Y. 21(1), 38–41.

Rosenthal, R., & Jacobson, L. (1968). *Pygmalion in the Classroom: Teacher Expectations and Pupils' Intellectual Development*. New York: Holt, Rinehart and Winston.

Rosin, H. (2010, July/August). *The Over Protected Kid*. *The Atlantic*. New York.

Rowen et al. (2007). "Choral Reading Theater: Bridging Accuracy Automaticity and Prosody in Reading Fluency Across an Academy Unit of Study." *Journal of Teacher Action Research*. Corpus Christi, TX.

Russell, P. (1979). *The Brain Book*. New York: E. P. Dutton.

Sadker, D., & Sadker, M. (1994) *Failing at Fairness: How Our Schools Cheat Girls*. Toronto, ON: Simon & Schuster Inc.

Sandseter, E. (2007) European Early Childhood Educational Research Journal, UK.

Schacter, D. L. (1996). *Searching for Memory: The Brain, Mind, and the Past*. New York: Basic Books.

Schank, R. C. (1990). *Tell Me a Story: Narrative and Intelligence*. Evanston, IL: Northwestern University Press.

Schmidt, S. R. (1995). Effects of humor on sentence memory. *Journal of Experimental Psychology: Learning, Memory and Cognition*, 20, 953–67.

Science Daily (2010). "Books in Home as Important as parent's Education in Determining Children's Educational level." Reno, NV: University of Nevada.

Schwarz, A. "The Selling of Attention Deficit Disorder." New York Times. Dec. 2013, New York.

Schwarz, A & Cohen, S. ADHD seen in 11% of US children as Diagnoses Rise. New York Times Company, New York, 2013.

Scientific Learning Corporation. (2016) *Fast ForWord Reading Language Program*. http://www.scientificlearning.com.

Shadmehr & Holcomb. (1997, August). Neural correlates of motor memory Consolidation. *Science Magazine*, 277.

Shearer, B. (2004). Multiple intelligences theory after 20 years. *Teachers College Record*, 106, 2–16.

Sherna N. (2012). Teenagers' Life Balance Revealed:17 hours weekly for T.V. and Another 17 hours for Internet. *Independent*, U.K.

Sigle-Rushton W, McLanahan S. "Father absence and child wellbeing: a critical review." In: Moynihan DP, Smeeding TM, Rainwater L, editors. The Future of the Family. New York: Russell Sage Found; 2004. pp. 116–55.

Skiba, Russel. (2006). *Are Zero Tolerance Policies Effective in the Schools?* A report by the American Psychological Association Task Force, 23–25.

Sortino, D. (2011). *The Promised Cookie—No Longer Angry Children*. Bloomington, IN: AuthorHouse.

Sousa, D. A. (2005). *How the Brain Learns to Read*. Thousand Oaks, CA: Corwin Press.

Sowell, E. R., Thompson, P. M., Holmes, C. J., Jernigan, T. L., & Toga, A. W. (1999). In-vivo evidence for post-adolescent brain maturation in frontal and striatal regions. *Nature: Neuroscience*, 2, 859–61.

Steinberg, L. (2005). Cognitive and effective development in adolescence. *Trends in Cognitive Sciences*, 9, 69–74.

Steiner, R. (1995). *The Kingdom of Childhood*. Dornech: Anthroposophic Press.

Stix, G. (2015). *Scientific American*. Armark, NY: Lake Group Media.

Strauss, L. (2011). *My Class Size Matters*. New York: Huffington Post.

Tokuhama-Espinosa, T. "Mind Brain and Educational Science: A comprehensive guide to the New Brain Based Teaching." New York: W.W. Norton and Company 2011.

Tokuhama-Espinosa, T. (2011). *Boys Are Not Made to Sit in Your Typical Classroom*. Mind Brain Education Science.

U.S. Department of Justice: Office of Juvenile Justice and Delinquency Prevention Programs 2000. Washington, D.C.

United States Department of Education. (2008) Washington, D.C.

Vaughn, K., & Winner, E. (2000). SAT scores of students who study the arts: What we can and cannot conclude about the association. *Journal of Aesthetic Education*, 34(3/4), 77–89.

Wadsworth, B. (1984). *Piaget's Theory of Cognitive And Affective Development* (3rd ed.). New York: Longman.

Wakefield, J. (2015). Children Spend Six hours or more a Day on Screens. BBC News. UK.

Wedge, M. (2012). Why French kids don't have ADHD. *Psychology Today*, Part 2, 1012.

Wahlstrom, K. "Examining the Impact of Later High School Start Times on the Health and Academic Performance of High School Students: A Multi-site Study." *College of Education and Human Development*. University of Minnesota. Feb. 2014. Minneapolis, MN.

Weinberger, N. M. (2004, November). Music and the brain. *Scientific American*, 291, 89–95.

Weisburg, D. (2006). *What Does Batman Think About Sponge Bob — Understanding of the Fantasy /Fantasy Distinction*. New York: In Cognition.

Wilson, V. et al. *Biofeedback*. Association for Applied Physiology and Biofeedback. In 2006. Wheat Ridge, CO. 34(3), 99.

Wixted, J. T. (2004). The psychology and neuroscience of forgetting. *Annual Review of Psychology*, 55, 235–69.

Wong,. A (2015) The Sesame Street Effect. *The Atlantic Monthly*, New York.

Wooden, J. (2009). *Game Plan for Life*. New York: Bloomsberg.

Wolfson, A., & Carskadon, M. (1998). Sleep schedules and daytime functioning in adolescents. *Child Development*, 69, 875–87.

About the Author

David P. Sortino, EdM, PhD, holds a Master's Degree in human development from Harvard University and a Doctorate in clinical psychology from Saybrook University, as well as multiple subject and learning handicapped teaching credentials. He has spent thirty-five years as a teacher, counselor, director, and resource specialist in public and private schools, as well as training teachers and counselors at the university level. He has served as consultant to state and county programs for at-risk youth and special needs children, and works directly with individuals and families.

In his private practice, he consults and collaborates with students, parents, teachers, and psychologists to provide support for students' pre-K through college in establishing school success and higher learning levels. He finds that exploring how the brain learns, as well as other learning strategies can help students develop a better understanding about how they learn in and out of the classroom. Currently, he directs The Neurofeedback Institute, writes a blog for the Santa Rosa Press Democrat, and hosts a bimonthly radio show called *Brain Smart—a Better learning Brain* on KOWS: 107.3. FM. He is the author of *The Promised Cookie: No Longer Angry Children*.

Made in the USA
Middletown, DE
13 March 2024

51312095R00097